A SHORT GUIDE TO ACADEMIC WRITING

Andrew P. Johnson

University Press of America,® Inc.
Lanham · New York · Oxford

Copyright © 2003 by
University Press of America,® Inc.
4501 Forbes Boulevard
Suite 200
Lanham, Maryland 20706
UPA Acquisitions Department (301) 459-3366

PO Box 317
Oxford
OX2 9RU, UK

Library of Congress Cataloging-in-Publication Data

Johnson, Andrew P. (Andrew Paul)
A short guide to academic writing / Andrew P. Johnson.
p.   cm.

Includes index.
1. English language—Rhetoric. 2. Academic writing.
I. Title.

PE1408.J68 2003   808'.042—dc21   2003040233 CIP

ISBN 0-7618-2503-7 (paperback : alk. ppr.)

A friend is someone who knows you well and is
willing to talk to you anyway.

This book is dedicated to my friend, Dr. Nat Pope.

Contents

SECTION THREE – THE PARTICULARS OF ACADEMIC WRITING

SECTION FOUR – SCIENCE AND RESEARCH

SECTION FIVE – FINAL PRODUCTS

Introduction

Anybody Can Write

Anybody can write. It is not something that only professors, grammarians, English teachers, and pseudo intellectuals drinking espresso in coffee shops can do. Writing is simply a matter of finding out what it is you have to say, organizing your thoughts, and putting the right words together to communicate your ideas. Below are four important ideas related to writing.

1. Anyone can write well. You become a better writer by practicing. If you do not write, you will not get better. As long as you keep writing, your writing will continue to improve no matter what age you are. I am a better writer this year than I was last year, not because I became smarter, but because I have done a great deal of writing and reading.

2. Reading improves your writing. Reading also improves your writing. It will increase your vocabulary, expand your knowledge base, and give you a feel for the sound and structure of language. Discipline yourself to pick up an expository text and read for ten minutes every day. This will help you become a better writer and improve your ability to read advanced textbooks. Also, you may learn something along the way.

3. All writers write poorly on their first drafts. Writers need to celebrate slop. Slop is the first step in producing a quality piece of writing. One of the many paradoxes in life is that you cannot write well unless you have first written poorly. The first draft of this chapter was a mess. But I threw those early drafts away. Nobody will ever see them. The version you are reading now has been revised at least fifteen times. I have let friends, colleagues, and editors read it to see how it plays in their heads. I have also read portions aloud into a tape recorder to get a sense of how it flows.

4. Learning to master academic writing is important. This book deals with an academic style of writing with which you may not be familiar. There are several reasons why learning to master this style of writing is important: First, whether it is right or not, people will make judgements about you based on your writing. Second, writing well increases the llikelihood that others will attend to your ideas. If you write poorly, your ideas become less credible. Third, if you cannot communicate your ideas in a concise, logical fashion, they will be forever trapped in your head. E-mail, memos, letters, brochures, handbooks, web pages, manuals all rely on written words to transport your thoughts from point A to point B. Finally, writing helps you organize your thinking.

Section One
The Process of Writing

Chapter 1

Writing Groups

An effective technique to get feedback on your work and to improve your writing skills is to form a writing group. Here, people meet in groups of three to eight to read and respond to each other's writing. (The most effective writing groups usually have four or five members.) You can form these groups as part of any class that involves writing. Or, if you are reading this text apart from a class, I would encourage you to create a writing group on your own.

Writing groups provide support and valuable feedback to members as they go through the academic writing process. Also, it is very common to lose perspective you have been working on. The writing group allows you to see how a piece of writing is playing in the heads of different readers.

Writing Group Sessions

Writing groups generally meet in a writing conference once a week. If you are involved in larger writing projects, meeting once every two weeks might be more comfortable. To be effective, all members must contribute equally, thus, it is important that each come to the writing conference prepared. In general, there are three approaches to use in responding to writing in a writing conference:

1. Oral comments. Members bring a piece of their writing to read aloud to the group. Members provide oral comments, ask questions, and make suggestions.

2. Read and respond before the writing conference. Here one or more members make copies of their writing for all group members. Members should be given these copies a minimum of two days before the writing conference (a week is best). This copy should be typed and doubled spaced to facilitate reading and allowing room for written comments. Feedback is given each paper in the form of written comments *before* the group meets.

At the conference, 10 to 15 minutes is spent on each member's paper. Members should describe strengths but also suggest possible changes. Feedback is an important part of the writing process. Giving and receiving honest feedback is the best way to improve as a writer.

3. Pass around the group during the conference. Group members bring one copy of an excerpt or a short piece of writing to pass around the group. During the conference, members make written comments on each and then pass them along as they finish. When all papers have been read by all group members, each person then receives general oral comments and suggestions by the group.

General Writing Conference Guidelines

How groups choose to respond to each other's paper in the writing conference is a matter of preference. Conferences generally last anywhere from 30 minutes to two hours. The feedback provided as part of conferences should be supportive but honest and explicit. The rating checklist in Figure 1.1 can be used to provide feedback.

Final Thoughts

Here are four final thoughts to keep in mind as you begin this journey toward improved academic writing: First, beginning drafts are works in progress. Second, bad writing is the first step toward good writing. Third, it is normal for people to be at different places with respect to their writing ability. And finally, there is no such thing as a perfect paper.

Figure 1.1. Rating checklist for academic writing.

Key: 3 = very much, 2 = some, 1 = little, 0 = not at all.

Criteria	Rating
1. Ideas: The writer creates interesting, relevant, novel, thoughtful, or unique ideas. These ideas are supported or explained.	
2. Sentences: The writer uses complete sentences. The sentences are (a) concise yet descriptive, (b) consistent with tense and plurality, (c) avoid repetition, and (d) make sense and are easy to read.	
3. Paragraphs: The writer uses paragraphs to break up and organize larger ideas. The paragraphs (a) make sense, (b) avoid conceptual leaps, and (c) are used to explore or support an idea.	
4. Word choice: The writer (a) uses an academic style, (b) avoids speech-isms or colloquialisms, and (c) makes pragmatic choices about the quantity and quality of words.	
5. Headings: The writer uses headings to organize the paper and make it reader-friendly. All the information under a particular heading is germane to that section.	
6. Quotes and citations: The writer uses APA form as described here. The quotes and citations are used intelligently to support the writer's ideas.	
7. Fluency: The piece flows and is easy to read. Ideas are described and supported.	
8. Structure/Organization: Structure is used to help carry the ideas.	
9. Form/Mechanics: The piece looks presentable. The spacings, margins, font, and headings are correct. Spelling, grammar, and punctuation have been attended to.	

10. Strengths of this paper:

11. Questions or areas to reconsider:

Chapter 2

Writing is a Very Messy Process

Your initial emphasis as a writer should be on the process of writing. What your writing should look like will come later.

The Process

Writing is a very messy process. All writers struggle for words, ideas, and organization initially. Very few of us are like Mozart, who could write music and get it exactly right the first time. Most of us are like Beethoven: we struggle, revise, and mess about until we discover exactly what it is we want to say and how we want to say it.

Avoid Writers' Block

Writers' block is a condition where the words and ideas just do not come out. And it seems as if the harder you try, the fewer words and ideas appear on the page. This comes from trying to get it just right the first time. Writing will be difficult and the quality will most likely be poor if you try to edit and generate your ideas simultaneously.

Writing involves two opposite mental operations: Generating and evaluating. You need to generate in order to get an abundance of words and ideas, but you also need to evaluate in order to throw out and reshape words and ideas you have generated. But you cannot do both of these operations at the same time. You cannot generate and evaluate simultaneously and expect to create anything but warm mush.

The reason for this has to do with the way our brains work. While our long term memory (LTM) can hold a great deal of information for an almost infinite duration, our short term memory (STM) or working memory can hold only about seven chunks of information for approximately 15 seconds. This is not much room for a great deal of information. If you try to edit and organize your ideas at the same time as you are generating ideas, STM becomes overloaded and many of the ideas seem to slip away or become scattered.

One of the best cures for writers' block is to use a pencil and a legal pad and write as quickly and as badly as possible. This technique allows you to bypass the little editor in your head so that you can get your initial ideas on paper. As described below, editing is the last step in the writing process.

Steps of the Writing Process

The steps described below describe the process that many writers have found to be effective.

Pre-Writing

The first step is to engage in some sort of pre-writing activity. What you do before you write is just as important as what you do as you are writing. I like to brainstorm and list. Here, I grab a yellow legal pad and start listing ideas as quickly as I can. After I have a paper filled with scratches and messy sentences, I look for patterns and groups and then begin to create an outline. Other pre-writing ideas include creating semantic webs, talking through ideas with friends, power-writing, and gathering data. These are described here:

Semantic webs. The semantic web allows you to generate ideas at the same time as you create structure. First, draw a circle in the middle of your paper and write your topic in the circle. Then, think of three or four ideas related to your topic. Each of these will become a node (see Figure 2.1). Next, list as many ideas as you can for each node. Finally, use this flexible structure to begin writing. Each node of your web will become sections or paragraphs.

Figure 2.1. Semantic web.

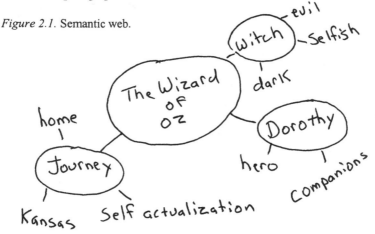

Talking. Explain your writing ideas to a friend. This helps to organize the ideas in your head and detect any missing parts. Encourage your friend to ask questions or add ideas.

Power writing. Power writing helps you get in touch with your unconscious. Starting with your writing topic, write as many things as quickly as you can for one to three minutes. The goal is to create many ideas, both good ones and bad ones. Do not let your pen stop moving. Free associate. Let your mind travel. Capture the first words that pop into your head. It does not matter if you jump from one idea to the next or if your ideas are jumbled. You will get it straightened out later.

Gathering data. If you are writing research or an expository piece of text, you must gather data before you begin to write. This data will shape what it is you have to say. Data gathering involves note-taking. Here, you will read journals, magazine articles, book chapters, observe, or conduct interviews. When you have collected all your data, begin to look for patterns or groups to put your data into.

First Draft - Sloppy Copy

A first draft becomes an external version of your STM and is used to hold your thoughts as you generate and organize them. The goal here is to get your first ideas on paper. If this first draft does not look messy and unorganized, then you have probably done it incorrectly.

Revision

Re-vision means seeing again. The first draft is like a sculptor throwing the first glob of clay on the wheel. Revision is where you begin to shape the clay. I know of no sculptor who would spin the wheel once or twice and consider the sculpture finished. There is always a great deal of shaping and reshaping. The same applies to your writing. Expect to revise a minimum of four times, but usually ten to fifteen times. Do not worry about spelling and punctuation here; rather, try to find a logical organization and listen to see if your sentences and paragraphs make sense.

Editing

This is the last step. Here, you will run your writing through a spell check program and concentrate on grammar, punctuation, word usage, and citations. It is also helpful to have others read your work at this stage. Often, you get so close to a piece of writing that you cannot see the simple errors.

Chapter 3

Reading Critically

This chapter describes: (a) reading and comprehension, (b) strategies to comprehend academic texts, and (c) the brain and comprehension.

Reading is Not the Same as Comprehending

Have you ever read a piece of text and afterwards find that you have no idea what it was you just read? Reading is different from comprehending. Comprehension is the act of creating meaning with a text (Dole, Duffy, Roehler, & Pearson, 1991). To comprehend, readers use the information in their head to filter, organize, and interpret the incoming information and to ultimately construct meaning (Fitzpatrick, 1994; Gunning, 1996). This means that you use what you know to make sense of what you read. If you know a great deal about a subject, it is much easier to read and comprehend. For example, I am able to read articles related to writing fairly quickly with a high rate of comprehension. However, when I try to read things about finance, the market, computers, or statistics, I find that I have to reread the text several times and take notes in order to comprehend.

Romance Novels and Academic Texts

You cannot read a college textbook or an article in an academic journal the same way as you read a novel or story. Very few people are able to read this kind of expository text through once and get a good idea of what it is they have just read. Most professors that I know usually read things through two and usually three times and use some type of comprehension strategy.

One key to comprehending what you read is to be actively involved somehow. Taking good notes is one of the best ways to understand and remember what you read. Here you can see your ideas laid out on paper and see how one thing is related to another. Also, taking notes when you read or listen to a lecture helps you to be actively involved. The act of picking out key ideas and recording them moves you from a passive receiver of ideas to an active processor of ideas.

Comprehension Strategies

There are many different strategies to use when reading and comprehending academic text. Find a strategy that works best for you.

Listed here are five strategies that can be used to improve comprehension:

Note Taking

1. Read quickly. Read the chapter or article quickly, and put a dot in the margin of the text to indicate interesting or important ideas. Try not to slow up during this stage as that will interrupt the flow and make it less likely that you will see how one thing relates to the other.

2. Highlight. Reread and highlight the sentences you have marked. A note of caution here: Be judicious in your use of highlighting. If you highlight an entire page of text, it does little to help you pick out the important ideas. If you are using a text from the library or if you are the kind of person who hates writing in a text, go directly to step 3. The advantage of the highlighted chapter is that you can reread the chapter or article fairly quickly simply by attending to the highlighted ideas.

3. Take notes. Now put your ideas in outline form using only one side of your notebook paper. The outline helps you see the main and supporting ideas and how they relate to the topic. Using only one side of your notebook page allows you to spread out your notes in front of you when you are creating your extremely rough first draft.

Pre-Reading

1. Look at the title.

2. Read the first paragraph.

3. Read the headings.

4. Read the last paragraph.

5. Read the article/chapter.

6. Take notes. When you begin note-taking, use an outline form. The chapter headings and subheadings should be used as organizing points in your notes.

Paragraph Re-Read

1. Read each paragraph quickly. The goal during the first reading is to get a gist of the paragraph, knowing that you will reread the paragraph to get the particulars.

2. Reread to find the important ideas.

3. Record the important ideas.

4. Continue.

Paragraph Summarizing

1. Read a paragraph.

2. Find the important ideas.

3. Summarize and take notes.

4. Record using your own words.

5. Continue.

Re-Read
   1. Read the entire article/chapter quickly.
   2. Reread the article/chapter.
   3. Note or record important ideas.

Using Your Brain to Comprehend

As new information is perceived, it is stored in short term memory (STM). Aa stated previously, STM has a very limited capacity, holding about seven chunks of information for approximately 15 seconds (Miller, 1956). It is here that the new information is processed and eventually stored in long term memory (LTM). LTM is like a gigantic file cabinet in our heads that holds a tremendous amount of information for an unlimited amount of time.

With human information processing systems, information flows two ways: First, it flows from perception to STM, where it is processed, and then to LTM, where it is stored. But information also flows the other way. Information stored in LTM is used to process information in STM and also to help humans perceive patterns or attend to important information around them. This means that humans use the information in their heads together with information perceived in the environment to help create or construct meaning.

The Frictionless Flow

Learning is a matter of using knowledge to build cognitive structures in LTM, which can then be used to solve problems and create products. Knowledge is best absorbed when there is an efficient, frictionless flow back and forth from perception to STM to LTM. The following study tips help in creating this frictionless flow:

   1. Take notes. Taking good notes frees up space in STM. The paper on which notes are written relieves STM of the burden of holding onto ideas as they are processed. And, as stated previously, taking notes helps you to become actively involved in constructing knowledge.

   2. Relax. Tension and anxiety interrupt the frictionless flow by taking up space in STM. There are a variety of tricks that can be used to help you relax in order to improve concentration such as reading something enjoyable, using deep breathing or a meditation technique, or studying in a place that you enjoy yet are not distracted. Some people use music to help them relax, however, music does not promote optimum concentration for reading and writing, and should be turned off eventually. Anxiety can be alleviated also by starting your projects long before they are due.

   3. Eliminate distractions. Find a quiet place with no distractions. STM must be free to concentrate only on the information you are reading or writing about.

4. Segment the task. It is easy to get overwhelmed if you have a great deal to read and write. Create an outline or a plan that segments the task into smaller bits. Give yourself plenty of time to accomplish the task, get started right away, and do a little bit every day. Also, give yourself little rewards after you complete each segment such as a candy bar, a coffee break, or a phone call.

5. Sleep. If you feel yourself getting tired, take a nap. Your brain has periods of high and low functioning during any given day. You cannot expect to get up in the morning and maintain peak efficiency for 10 to 15 hours. Even taking 10 minutes to close your eyes, relax, and think of nothing will refresh your brain and improve concentration. Tired brains simply do not function as well as fresh, rested brains.

6. Eat well and eat light. Without proper nutrition, it is hard for any part of your body to operate at peak efficiency. However, if you eat too much, the blood used for concentration goes to the stomach to aid in digestion. Just like athletic performance, light carbohydrates seem to help one achieve peak writing performance.

7. Spread out the task. This is very much related to segmenting the task. If you engage in small bits of writing spread out over time, you will spend far less time and energy. This also provides your subconscious the opportunity to manipulate the ideas and thus, helps you create a better writing product. If you try to overwhelm your brain with massive amounts of writing in a short period of time, you will spend far more time and energy and have a much poorer writing product.

8. Read. Get in the habit of reading. Find things that you enjoy reading such as newspapers, magazines, novels, or nonfiction books. One becomes a better reader only by reading. Reading of any kind enhances your vocabulary, improves your ability to recognize words and sentences, and increases reading fluency. Also, reading provides you an implicit sense of grammar and sentence structure.

References

Dole, J., Duffy, G., Roehler, L., Pearson, P.D. (1991). Moving from the old to the new: Research on reading comprehension instruction. *Review of Educational Research, 61*, 239-264.

Fitzpatrick, K. (1994). Improving reading comprehension using critical thinking strategies. *Reading Improvement, 31*, 142-144.

Gardner, H. (1983). Frames of mind. New York: HarperCollins.

Gunning, T.G. (1996). *Creating reading instruction for all children.* Needham Heights, MA: Allyn & Bacon.

Miller, G.A. (1956). The magical number seven, plus or minus two:
    Some limits on our capacity for processing information.
    Psychological Review, 63, 81-97.

Chapter 4

Sources and Notes

Academic Writing Uses Credible Sources

Academic journals are the best source for academic writing. These contain articles written by specialists in the field that describe research, secondary research, novel applications of existing theories, or new or interesting ideas set in a theoretical context. There are hundreds of different academic journals in all areas, from medicine to psychology, cosmetology, and farming.

It Is Not a Magazine

An academic journal is not the same as a magazine. Magazines are designed to attract a wide audience and make a profit for the publisher. They are usually written by a staff of writers or reporters who often do not have an expertise in the fields about which they are reporting. It is hard to report accurately about a subject with which you have little knowledge, thus, accuracy is often compromised here. Also, magazines depend on advertising revenue, which does affect the kinds of things that are published.

Academic journals are designed to inform the field. They do not employ a staff of writers. Instead, scientists, researchers, teachers, and other academicians send in their work to be considered for publication. Each article is peer reviewed, which means it is critiqued by a jury of three to six experts in the field to check for accuracy and validity. Each reviewer then makes a recommendation whether or not to accept the article for publication. Often there are many revisions made before an article is finally accepted for publication. Also, academic journals contain little or no advertising, and the authors list all their sources at the end of each article.

Books

Books are credible sources also, however, just because it is written in some book does not make it true. Books that cite their sources and those published by major publishing houses can generally be trusted to provide credible information.

How to Gather Data Using Credible Sources

You should look for as many recent credible sources as possible (published within the last five years). It is common to spend a great deal of time during the beginning stages of a writing project simply reading articles and taking notes. While this may seem to be very time consuming initially, you will be able to write much faster and with greater ease during the writing stages.

These are the steps used to gather data using credible sources:

Step 1: Find a Good College Library

A public library will not have the academic journals and books needed to complete your paper. The internet is a good place to find information initially; however, this information is often not very credible. That is, anybody can write and publish things on the internet. Journal articles on the other hand, are reviewed before being published. Until there is a system whereby information on the internet is peer-reviewed, edited books and academic journals are your best sources of data. (There are a few peer-reviewed journals currently on the internet.)

Step 2: Locate Possible Sources

The library you use will have some type of computer-based system in which all its journal articles are entered by key words. There will be another database in which the books contained at that library are categorized and described. I recommend using journal articles over books whenever possible as they are more current, more focused, and allow you to get a great amount of information from a variety of sources in a short amount of time. To locate your sources, enter the title or subject related to your topic. Libraries use various ways to organize books and academic journals.

For academic journals, you will be provided the name of the journal, the volume, the number, and the page number. It will look something like this:

Johnson, A. (1998). What exactly are comprehension skills and how do I teach them? *Reading, 32,* 22-26.

This tells me the author (Johnson, A.), the year the article was published (1998), the title of the article (What Exactly are Comprehension Skills and How Do I Teach Them?), the name of the journal (Reading), the volume (32), and the page numbers on which it can be found (pages 22-26). Most libraries organize their journals and magazines alphabetically by journal title. These are the easiest to find. Once you locate the journal, the year and volume number should be listed on the front cover. When journals are two or more years old, libraries usually take all the journals from a particular year or volume and bind them in book form. This makes the journals easier to find and helps them last longer.

For example, to find the article above I would go to the "R" section of the journals and magazines until I found the journal, *Reading*. Then, I would look for the volume number 32 (there will be several *Reading* journals listed as volume 32), and find the second journal (number 2) published within that volume. The article I want will be found on page 22 of that journal.

Sometimes, journals are organized by Library of Congress number. That number will look something like this:

LB 1011. R2.

Here I would go to the journals found in the "L" section. These will all be journals of similar topics. Then I would move down until I found the "LB" section, then the "1101s," and finally, "1101.R2".

Books may be organized either by Library of Congress numbers or the Dewy Decimal number. If you do not know how to do this, find a librarian.

Step 3: Peruse Your Sources

After you get a pile of books or journals, find a table and take a few minutes to see if your sources will provide you with information related to your question. For books, check the table of contents and the index and then scan a few chapters. For journal articles, read the abstract and scan the headings, subheadings, and final paragraph. A few minutes here will save you much time later on as well as saving you from having to carry around a pile of books and journals.

Step 4: Take Careful Notes

When taking notes, first record the full reference citation at the top of the page (this will be explained in the next chapter). Having the citation here will save you the task of having to look up the articles again when creating the reference page. Next, record your notes using only one side of the page. This allows you to spread all your notes out in front of you when you begin to write your first draft.

To illustrate how your notes should look, I have included some of the notes that I used in writing an article about reading comprehension (Johnson, 1998). Here, I only recorded the information that was needed to support my topic question: How can we help children comprehend expository text? These notes were written using short sentences, which were often incomplete. The goal during note-taking is not to create grammatically correct writing; rather, to restate and remember the author's ideas in a way that makes them readily accessible to you.

NOTES FOR COMPREHENSION ARTICLE

Fitzpatrick, K. (1994). Improving reading comprehension using critical thinking strategies. *Reading Improvement, 31*, 142-144.
1. Critical thinking strategies can be used to improve comprehension.
2. Teachers can focus on strategies which require students to think critically.
3. Reading comprehension = reader constructs meaning while interacting with printed page.
4. Critical thinking = determining the value of an idea, concept, or solution.
5. Divergent thinking should also be encouraged along with critical thinking.
6. Any strategy in which the students converse is valuable.

Dole, J.A., Duffy, G.G., Roehler, L.R., & Pearson, P.D. (1991). Moving from the old to the new: Research on reading comprehension instruction. *Review of Educational Research, 61*, 239-264.
1. Interactive approach - Uses students' knowledge and strategies to interpret text.
2. Knowledge - many forms: (a) knowledge about topic, (b) general world knowledge, (c) knowledge about organization of text, and (d) knowledge about strategies.
3. Expert readers have a set of flexible strategies that they use to make sense of the text and monitor their understanding.
4. Comprehension is more strategies than skills.
5. Strategies are conscious, flexible plans readers apply and adapt to various text.
6. Skill are high routinized, almost automatic behavior.

Step 5: The Next Step
The next step is to look for groups and begin writing a rough first draft. This will be explained in later chapters.

The Reference Page
You will notice that this chapter has a reference section at the end. In your writing, any article or book that is referred to in the text, must appear on the reference page at the end. In academic books, references are found at the end of each chapter or at the end of the book. This allows the reader to see what sources the author used and to locate those sources if necessary. For example, when I was writing an article on reading

comprehension (Johnson, A.), I saved time locating sources by looking up the references and reading the articles that were cited in the articles that I read. Thus, by reading one article, I was able to get good information as well as to find other possible sources.

References

Johnson, A. (1998). What exactly are comprehension skills and how do I teach them? *Reading, 32,* 22-26.

Dole, J.A., Duffy, G.G., Roehler, L.R., & Pearson, P.D. (1991). Moving from the old to the new: Research on reading comprehension instruction. *Review of Educational Research, 61*, 239-264.

Fitzpatrick, K. (1994). Improving reading comprehension using critical thinking strategies. *Reading Improvement, 31*, 142-144.

Chapter 5

Taking Notes

This chapter describes (a) what your notes should look like and (b) how to organize your notes and write an extremely rough first draft.

What Your Notes Should Look Like

Below are some of the notes I used when writing the comprehension article referred to in an earlier chapter (Johnson, 1998). They are included here so that you might get a sense of this important step in the academic writing process. In these notes, notice how short, abbreviated sentences are used to paraphrase or capture the idea. The outline or list form helps me to quickly see the ideas, the structure of the whole, and how one idea is related to another. This form also makes it much easier to see the patterns or groups emerge during the drafting stage.

Gunning, T.G. (1996). *Creating reading instruction for all children*. Needham Heights, MA: Allyn & Bacon

1. Comprehension uses knowledge.
2. Comprehension is making connection between what we know and what we don't.
3. Reader plays an active role in constructing meaning.
4. 5 kinds of strategies: (a) preparation, (b) organization, (c) elaboration, (d) rehearsing, and (e) summarizing.

Strategies
1. Preparing = survey texts and predict.
2. Organizing = constructing relationship between ideas in the text.
A. Main ideas and supporting details, classifying, making groups.
B. Paraphrasing, summarizing, clustering related words, noting and using text
3. Elaboration = build associations between information in head and text.
A. Drawing inferences, creating analogies, visualizing.
4. Rehearsing = Taking steps to remember information.
5. Monitoring = being aware of one's comprehension and regulating it.
A. Set goals, adjust speed.

Dole, J., Duffy, G., Roehler, L., & Pearson, P.D. (1991). Moving from the old to the new: Research on reading comprehension instruction. *Review of Educational Research, 61,* **239-264.**

1. Takes cog. view of reading comprehension, from cognitive psychology.
2. Reader constructs meaning with text.
3. Information in head mixes with information on page.
4. Knowledge is an important part of comprehending.
 A. Use knowledge to filter and organize information.
5. Can apply strategies: Conscious, flexible, high level, instantaneous plans readers apply to various texts (see Pressley).
6. Skill is performed automatically without conscious attention.
 A. Strategy is just the opposite.
7. Strategies imply metacognitive awareness.
8. Traditional view of reading sees a passive reader employing skills.
9. Cog. view of reading = active reader, constructing meaning using flexible strategies to foster, monitor, and maintain comprehension.
What Skills Should be Taught
* Goal of strategy instruction is to dev. a set of strategies that can be adapted to any text.
 1. Strategy 1 - Determining importance.
 A. In school, usually this means author-based decisions vs. student based decisions.
 B. Can be improved thru instruction. (Ordering)
 2. Strategy 2 - Summarizing info.
 A. Sift through text, differentiate and order, create a coherent now.
 B. Select, condense, integrate info.
 3. Strategy 3 - Drawing inferences.
 A. Use to fill ind details in what we read.
 B. Teach how to integrate prior knowledge.
 4. Strategy 4 - Generate questions.
 A. Deep level processing (Lockhart).
 B. Generate your own question prior to reading (KWL or during reading (Reciprocal teaching.)
 5. Strategy 5 - Monitoring comprehension.
 A. Read and pause.

Organizing Notes: Looking for Groups

Once you have carefully read your articles and taken notes, the next step is to package the ideas so that they can be easily understood by your reader. This means putting the ideas into groups or categories.

Groups Emerge

Spread your notes out on a table so you can see them all. When I did this with the notes above, the following groups or categories began to emerge: (a) knowledge, (b) creating meaning, (c) strategies, skills, tactics, and (d) successful and unsuccessful readers. I then began to move the ideas from my notes into groups with a code to remember where I got each idea from so that I would be able to cite it later. For example, G96 is a code for Gunning, 1996 and D91 is a code for Dole, Duffy, Roehler, & Pearson, 1991. Below is an example of how I began to group ideas in the knowledge category.

Knowledge

1. Comprehension uses knowledge (G 96).
 A. Comprehension is making connection between what we know and what we don't know.
2. Comprehension depends heavily on knowledge (FP, 94).
3. Knowledge is an important part of comprehending (D91).
 A. Use to filter and organize information.
4. New knowledge helps the comprehension practice (F, 94).
5. Reviewing background helps with comprehension (FP 94).

Extremely Rough First Draft

As I put each idea into a group, I used a highlight marker to cross it off. Once all my ideas were in groups I was then ready to begin constructing an extremely rough first draft. Again, if you try to get your paragraphs just right at this stage, you will clog up the writing mechanism. Also, as you continue to revise, you will be moving many of your ideas around and throwing away much of what you write, therefore, it makes little sense to polish. There will be time enough for this during the final revising stages.

Knowledge is an important part of comprehension during the reading process (G, 96; FP, 94 ; D, 91). Readers use the knowledge in their head to help understand what they read. This knowledge is used to filter and organize incoming data, as well as make connections between the new and the old.

The Final Draft

The paragraph above is an extremely rough first draft. You are the only ones who have ever seen one of my paragraphs in such rough form. I quickly slapped this together and moved on, knowing that I would be coming back to shape it later. In this case, I eventually added some things and took others out. The final draft is shown below. Notice how different it is from the first draft.

Comprehension is the act of constructing meaning with a text (Dole et al., 1991). Here, readers take an active role, using information in their head to filter, organize, interpret, and generate relationships with the incoming information and to ultimately construct meaning (Fielding & Pearson, 1994; Fitzpatrick, 1994; Gunning, 1996).

References

Cunning, P.M, Moore, S.A., Cunningham, J.W., & Moore, D.W. (1995). *Reading and writing in elementary classrooms: Skills and observations* (3rd ed.). White Plains, NY: Longman.

Dole, J., Duffy, G., Roehler, L., & Pearson, P.D. (1991). Moving from the old to the new: Research on reading comprehension instruction. *Review of Educational Research, 61*, 239-264.

Fielding, L.G. & Pearson R.D. (1994). Reading comprehension: What works. *Educational Leadership, 31*, 62-68.

Fitzpatrick, K. (1994). Improving reading comprehension using critical thinking strategies. *Reading Improvement, 31*, 142-144.

Gunning, T.G. (1996). *Creating reading instruction for all children.* Needham Heights, MA: Allyn & Bacon.

Johnson, A. (1998). What exactly are comprehension skills and how do I teach them? *Reading, 32,* 22-26.

Rabren, K., & Darch, C. (1996). The strategic comprehension behaviors of students with learning disabilities and general education students. *Journal of Research and Development in Education, 29,* 172-180.

Chapter 6

Writing With Your Unconscious

Your Unconscious Mind is Your Friend

I have paused here. This chapter was not happening the way I wanted it to when I first set about to write it. I had much to say, but the words seemed to splatter onto the page like a disjointed Robert Pollack painting. When I read back what I had written, it all seemed so very wrong.

The problem was, I was thinking too much. This excess of logical thought made it very hard for my conscious mind to access the wealth of ideas bubbling in my unconscious. I needed to find a way to connect my conscious and unconscious mind.

Power Write

The power-write, as discussed briefly in Chapter 1, is an excellent way to tap into the power of your unconscious mind as you write. For my power-write I grabbed a pencil and legal pad, opened up a writing text, found an interesting idea to use to prime the pump, and started writing. I wrote down the first thing that popped into my mind. The ideas that began to appear on the page were strange and disjoined, however, I started to get a sense of where I wanted to go with this chapter. And the more I wrote, the more the ideas seemed to flow onto the page. In about seven minutes I had three pages of scribbled notes, words, sentences, half-sentences, and even diagrams. Much of what I wrote was garbage; however, in that pile of garbage were three very good ideas that I had not considered before. Also, out of my pile of garbage I began to see the necessary structure for this chapter. My conscious mind could see how the parts might be put together to create a logical whole.

Your unconscious mind is your writing ally. Undisturbed by conscious contamination, ideas grow here like bacteria in a petri dish. Listed below are three other techniques to use in order to tap into the power of your unconscious mind:

Take a Nap

It is difficult for most people to operate at peak mental efficiency for eight to ten hours straight. I find that a ten to twenty-minute power nap enables my conscious mind to become more refreshed and revitalized and in the process, allows my unconscious mind to burp up ideas that are lingering there.

Do Something Else

Leave your writing for a day or two and then come back. While you are off doing other things, your unconscious mind is still hard at work. This is why I encourage my students in my writing course to start their papers early in order to allow for some good unconscious percolating time.

Think About Nothing

A good way to think about something is to think about nothing. I know this sounds strange and mystical, but it really works. To do this, find a quiet place where you can sit, relax, and get comfortable. Next, close your eyes, and begin to take long, slow, rhythmic breaths. With each breath, picture the air coming in through your nose, filling your body, and then leaving. Finally, empty your mind by thinking of a nonsense word such as "abba-dabba," or "in-out." Repeat this phrase with every inhalation and exhalation. Nature abhors a vacuum, and the vacuum you create will quickly be filled by a multitude of ideas.

The Bone Pile

Having too many words is just as dangerous to comprehension as having too few words. Many times when writing and revising I find that I have too many words on the page and these sentences impede the flow of ideas. However, it is very difficult for me to throw things away once I have worked so hard to write them. A psychological trick I use in this situation is called the bone pile. Here I cut out those things that I think I can do without and move them down to the very bottom of the page in what I call the bone pile. This is a pile of discarded sentences and paragraphs. This gets them out of the way so I can see what I am working with, but it still allows me the opportunity to go back and retrieve them if necessary. Included below is my sample bone pile for this chapter. This bone pile is a garbage dump for old discarded ideas and thus, it should make little sense to you.

Sample Bone Pile

- What about quotes? I recommend that students use quotations very judiciously. If you lift large blocks of text and quote a great deal, suddenly you lose your voice. Instead of you we hear a series of other people

- Sticking with the idiot theme... Know that short words and sentences are easier to understand and follow than longer ones, so you need to remember that when writing your sentences, you always check to make sure they do not go on and on endlessly as it becomes tiresome to the reader and loses your point.

- Words that do not exactly fit are more apt to cause your message not to be read or understood.

- But, I did go back and research the writing manuals, as well as my own class notes to see what information I needed to convey about developing a sense of audience.

- if that's your goal ...

- Beginning academic writers often do not have a good sense of how their words should sound. With a great deal of writing practice, you will eventually develop a writer's ear for the sound of the written language.

- Listening to your own writing this way will always result in clarification for you.

Section Two
Academic Writing

Chapter 7

What is Academic Writing?

I walked from the rustic cabin, down the cool, quiet forest path that lead to the lake. It was early morning. The tall trees created a rich, green canopy above me. The green, leafy underbrush reached out to welcome me. Up ahead I could see the sun exploding on the surface of the water. Joy welled up inside me. It was summer and I had three months to swim in the clear, blue lake, play tennis with Ralph and Sue, and hike the trails.

Andy spent the summer at Wood Lake swimming, playing tennis, and hiking.

Form and Function

The type of writing used in academic settings is different from creative writing in both purpose and form. The purpose of creative writing is to communicate metaphorically, generate images and emotions, or to entertain. This writing has a myriad of forms, is usually longer, and often contains dialogue. Here the writer is able to inject his or her insights and emotions. Academic writing is used to communicate ideas. This writing is more formal, uses structure to carry the ideas, seldom contains dialogue, and is purposefully objective.

This is not meant to demean creative writing. I enjoy writing short stories, poetry, and philosophical kinds of pieces where I can use symbols and metaphors; however, academic writing is concise and objective. (There is a place for the subjective voice. This will be described in the next chapter.) You must take yourself out of it and let the ideas carry the paper. Good academic writing is like a new Dodge Neon without any extras (air conditioning, radio, automatic transmission, power brakes, or steering).

A Few Basics to Begin

1. Do not use contractions. Eliminate contractions from your academic and professional writing. Write like the character, Data on *Star Trek Next Generation* speaks.

2. Do not use useless adjectives. Adjectives are describing words that add life and vitality to a piece of creative writing; however, there is a fine line between vitality and subjective insight. If there are too many adjectives in a piece of academic and professional writing, we begin to see the writer more than the writing.

3. Provide just the facts. What exactly are the facts? What are the opinions? What are the personal insights? Give your readers just the facts and trust them to come to their own conclusion.

The Prime Directive

The prime directive in academic and professional writing is clear communication. This means that your ideas are presented in a logical, orderly manner so that the reader is able to gain the maximum of understanding with the minimum of time and effort. To achieve this effect, you must use structure and organization so that one thing leads to or is built upon another. Headings, punctuation, transition words, and phrases are all used to maintain a harmonious flow of thought from the first sentence to the last.

A Question

Before writing, put your topic in the form of one or more questions. This helps to create writing that is focused and has a logical structure. It will also help you in gathering and organizing your ideas. For example, Susan, one of my students, was very much interested in writing about using invented spelling for elementary students. Having first identified a topic, she then created the following three questions: What is invented spelling? How does it work? Is it effective?

Once she had put her topic in the form of these questions, she found it much easier to write. Everything in Susan's paper then related directly to these three questions.

A Few More Basics

1. Font: 12 point.

2. Font face: Times, Times New Roman, or Helvetica.

3. Margins: one inch on the top, bottom, and sides.

4. Page number: bottom center without a running head or top right with a running head. A running head is an abbreviated version of the title of your paper.

Chapter 8

Using Objective and Subjective Language

I touched on this briefly in the last chapter, but in academic writing, the writer usually maintains an objective stance. There are, however, many instances where the subjective stance is appropriate and these are described in the last part of this chapter. Objective means you are impartial. Even though your position may be highly subjective, let the ideas and information speak for themselves. You must appear to be an unbiased presenter of information. This creates a much stronger paper. For example, look at the two paragraphs below:

Less effective: In my opinion, *The Wizard of Oz* is the best movie ever made. I really like the story line because it is so well developed. And who can forget all the memorable characters? The music and dance numbers are fantastic and help to produce an effect which I found very enjoyable.
More effective: *The Wizard of Oz* is a classic movie. The story line is strong, the characters are well developed, and the music and dance numbers add greatly to the overall effect.

The second example contains just the statements and supporting ideas. I am much more apt to listen to this because the writer has not let his or her opinions get in the way of the ideas. This very subjective opinion is presented in an objective way and thus, the reader is much more apt to be persuaded. An objectively stated argument will allow for the objective processing of that information.

Avoid Letter-To-The-Editor Syndrome

Sometimes writers develop *letter-to-the-editor syndrome* and begin using highly charged statements and emotional buzzwords. This style of writing weakens your argument and persuades only those who are already persuaded. Those who agree with your position will continue to agree, while those who have a different position will be put off.

Less effective: I really believe that congress should pass an amendment against the disgusting act of burning the American flag. This outrageous behavior is an insult to our brave men and women who have died for our great nation.

Concise, well-supported statements will always produce a more powerful and persuasive argument.

More effective: Congress should pass an amendment against flag burning out of respect for those who have died in the service of our country.

Avoid Value Statements

It is more effective to create sentences that state an idea and then support it. This avoids the use of value statements. A value statement is where you say what you believe without offering support. Even if a sentence does reflect your values, it can be made stronger by taking out value words such as 'must', 'should', and 'needs to be'. Instead, state the idea and support it.

Less effective: Teachers really should use ability groups.
More effective: Using ability groups helps teachers meet the needs of all students.

Less effective: A study by Smith (1998) reveals a startling statistic: students spend an average of only 10 minutes a day in authentic reading experiences.
More effective: A study by Smith (1998) showed that students spend an average of 10 minutes a day in authentic reading experiences. Increasing this substantially will enhance students' reading abilities.

Less effective: Educators need to recognize other forms of intelligence.
More effective: Recognizing other forms of intelligence will help educators develop the full potential of all their students.

The Subjective Stance

There are places where the subjective stance is appropriate. These are described below:

The essay. In some essays your thoughts, experiences, and perspectives are an integral part of the paper.

Your research. When you are reporting your own study, you should refer to yourself instead of 'the researcher'.

Less effective: For this study, the researcher was looking for a school in a rural setting.
More effective: For this study, I was looking for a school in a rural

setting.

Ethnographic research methods. In doing qualitative or ethnographic studies, the researcher becomes the lens through which a bit of reality is interpreted. In these instances, the researcher states any biases up front, describes how data were collected, presents the data, and makes conclusions based on the data. Here, the researcher is an important part of the research.

Writing about your experiences. In writing about your experiences you would, of course, include yourself.

Using anecdotes or observations. Sometimes, you can create a stronger paper and make a point come to life by including your experiences, insights, or anecdotes.

Chapter 9

Writing and Speech

Writing is different from speech. Because of its permanence and one-way nature, writing is more elaborate and orderly than speech. Writing allows us to examine our thoughts so they can be tested, analyzed, shaped, evaluated, edited, sorted, and ordered before they are delivered. Once delivered, these thoughts become frozen in time.

Speech is impermanent and is usually accompanied by an interaction with another human (hopefully). Speech consists of shorter sentences, is less formal, and is not as organized as writing. The advantage of speech is that we can see our intended audience, judge the reaction or reception to our words, and make immediate adjustments. The disadvantage of speech is that it hangs our words out in the air without the chance to examine or retract them.

Writing and Thinking

Writing might be more closely compared to thinking. Writing shapes how we think, and thinking shapes how we write; however, writing is not the same as thinking. At the deepest level, we think in images and feelings. The words we put together can never be more than an approximation of our thoughts.

Avoid Speech-isms

Avoid colloquialisms or speech-isms. Academic writing should not sound like people talking. Here are some examples of common speech-isms to avoid:

1. *"As likely as not . . . "*
Less effective: This will as likely as not produce a great explosion.
More effective: This will likely produce a great explosion.

2. *"Without a doubt . . . "*
Less effective: This is without a doubt, the most interesting scene in the movie.
More effective: This is the most interesting scene in the movie.

3. *"I can tell you that . . . "*
Less effective: I can tell you that movies need to have big promotional budgets in order to succeed.

More effective: Movies need to have big promotional budgets in order to succeed.

4. *"What can I say but . . . "*
Less effective: What can I say but go see this movie.
More effective: Go see this movie.

5. *"I might add that . . . "*
Less effective: I might add that this movie will make you laugh.
More effective: Also, this movie will make you laugh.

6. *"It should be pointed out that . . . "*
Less effective: It should be pointed out that Shirley Temple was the first choice to play Dorothy in this movie.
More effective: Shirley Temple was the first choice to play Dorothy in this movie.

Avoid Non-Words

A non-word is one that does not need to be there. If a word is not needed, do not use it. Too many words get in the way of your message.

Less effective: Basically, what they needed was more time.
Less effective: In essence, what they needed was more time.
Most effective: They needed more time.

Chapter 10

Writing as Teaching

Anybody can make the obvious seem complex. Good writers are like good teachers in that they make the complex seem obvious. To do this, you must assume the reader knows nothing about your writing topic. This keeps you from creating gaps or conceptual leaps in your writing. It also forces you to fully analyze what it is you want to say. Below I am describing a wrestling move.

Less effective: When looking for a single-leg, shoot in hard with your head up. Don't shoot from too far out or your opponent will drive your head and do a step-over. You can attack at three levels: high, middle, or low. Each one should be set up before shooting. Get your opponent moving before you shoot. Make sure your front foot is on the outside and your head is on the inside, then lift and drive.

To which you reply, "Huh?"

More effective: The single-leg is an effective move to use in taking your opponent to the mat. The move starts in a wrestling stance (on the balls of your feet, elbows in, head up, slight crouch) and consists of five steps: First, set up the move by grabbing your opponents' head or shoulder and using steady pressure to gently push back. Second, as soon as you feel your opponent pressure into you, plant your back foot, lower your head and shoulders, and drive to the leg. Third, plant your front foot on the outside of your opponent's leg and grab the leg tightly with your head on the inside. Fourth, lift the leg up. Finally, with your head still on the inside of the elevated leg, drive your shoulder straight down through your opponent's thigh. Since you are holding the supporting leg, your opponent should fall to the mat.

Two Points
There are two things to notice in the second paragraph above: (a) I was gender neutral and (b) I used numerical organizing words.
Gender Neutral
You must be gender neutral in all your writing. The opponent above could have been male or female. Below are three tricks to use in avoiding

gender bias in your writing:

> *Trick #1:* Use plurals whenever possible.

> **Incorrect:** A writer must decide which prewriting strategy he will use.
> **Correct:** Writers must decide which prewriting strategy they will use.
> (Notice that 'writers' is plural so 'they' must also be plural.)
> **Better yet**: Writers must decide which prewriting strategy to use.

> *Trick #2:* Do not use pronouns.

> **Incorrect:** When a writer is beginning to write a report, he should make sure he has enough information.
> **Correct:** When beginning to write, it is important to have enough information.
> **Better yet**: It is important to have enough information before beginning to write.

> *Trick #3:* Use 'that person'.

> **Incorrect**: When a writer gets writers' block, he should use a prewriting strategy to generate ideas.
> **Correct:** When a writer gets writers' block, that person should use a prewriting strategy to generate ideas.
> **Better yet**: Using prewriting strategies to generate ideas will often eliminate writers' block.

Using 's/he' or 'he or she' should be avoided if possible. These are messy and cumbersome.

Numerical Organizing Words

Numerical organizing words (NOW) can be used to help the reader follow along when there are several points to be made or when something is described in sequential order. First, tell how many points are to be made (see the example below). Then, use the words, 'first', 'second', 'third' etc., to begin each point. This allows you to add a sentence or two of elaboration without confusing the reader. For example:

> There are four reasons why college students should learn to write well: First, those who are able to present their ideas in an orderly and interesting fashion are likely to get better grades. These writers are viewed as knowledgeable, credible students. Second, writing can be used to help organize thinking. Putting ideas on paper allows writers to look at

several items at one time without taxing short term memory. Third, people are more apt to attend to writing which is written in a concise, organized fashion. And finally, effective writing and communicating skills make graduating students a more valuable commodity on the job market.

Note that 'firstly', 'secondly', 'thirdly', etc., are not to be used. Also, if you have just a few items to present, you can use other kinds of organizing words such as 'next', 'after', 'while', 'also', and 'since'. However, make sure the beginnings of each sentence are varied.

Less effective: There are five steps to use in getting a paper started: First, decide on a topic. Then, brainstorm to generate ideas. Then, look for groups or patterns to use in organizing your ideas. Then, arrange your ideas into groups. Finally, use the first draft to get all the ideas on paper.
More effective: There are five steps to use in getting a paper started: First, decide on a topic. Then, brainstorm to generate ideas. Next, look for groups or patterns to use in organizing your ideas. After this, arrange your ideas into groups. Finally, use the first draft to get all the ideas on paper.

People Who Need People
It is easy to get too close to your writing and forget that while you may understand what you are saying and how one idea flows to the next, the reader may not. Get other people to read your paper. They will provide you with an outside perspective and help you to develop a sense of audience. All authors do this.

When providing feedback to another writer, let the writer know how the paper is playing inside your head. When you are reading, look for these things: (a) sentences that sound funny, (b) areas where you get mixed up, confused, or cannot follow the writer's thinking, (c) parts that you like, (d) parts that you want to know more about, (e) ideas that pop into your head as you read, (f) ideas to add to the paper, and (g) grammatical or spelling errors.
Say It and Support It
Once stated, your idea must be supported, explained, or elaborated. A sentence with supporting or elaborating sentences is what makes a paragraph. Paragraphs help to organize thinking and communicate ideas. An unsupported sentence results in a jumble of ideas that seem to be randomly slapped together. Below is an example of jumbleness:

Less effective: Prewriting is an important part of the writing process. Revising is the key to effective writing. But to write effectively, you must use objective, academic language. Anybody can write. Also, reading a lot helps our writing.

These are all lovely ideas, but unless you are psychotic, the paragraph makes little sense. (If it does make sense, see your doctor immediately.) Each one of these ideas should become a paragraph. Below is an example of a paragraph with supporting or elaborating ideas:

More effective: Using a prewriting strategy helps to create a better paper. These strategies allow writers to focus solely on generating ideas before trying to write or shape them. Often, during this idea-generation stage, writers are able to tap into their unconscious and generate ideas of which they were not consciously aware. Also, with a list of possible ideas on the paper, writers are often able to see the structure of their paper and thus, write a more organized paper in a shorter amount of time. Those who experience writers' block usually have not used a prewriting strategy.

Chapter 11

Creating Structure

Structure in writing is the skeleton used to carry your ideas. Outlines or semantic webs are two ways to create structure. These can be used both before and after you gather data.

Create Structure After Data-Gathering

If you do not know much about your writing topic, you will need to collect data before you begin to think about structure. Collecting data includes reading articles or chapters and taking concise, paraphrased notes, and also generating ideas via brainstorming or power writes.

The beginning of your writing is like the beginning of a universe. First, gather data. Second, scatter your notes out in front of you. Create a chaotic field of your recorded ideas. Third, within the chaos, look for common ideas. Common ideas will be drawn together to create sections (two to five sections will suffice for most papers). These beginning sections will be like developing planets orbiting around the sun (your topic). Fourth, within each section, look for similar items for paragraphs or subsections (these will be the moons orbiting around your planets). Finally, within each paragraph, begin to create sentences.

Outline or Web Before Data-Gathering

If you are fairly knowledgeable about your writing topic, you can create a flexible outline or web before you begin collecting data. This outline or web will guide you in the data collection phase. However, keep this initial outline flexible; allow for new data to shape your work.

Headings and Subheadings

Structure makes it much easier to read your paper, however to be of use, the structure must be readily apparent. Writers want to avoid large blobs of text without headings or subheadings. Below is a blob of text. Generally, blobs of text are hard to read because the structure in indistinct.

The Wizard of Oz

The Wizard of Oz is considered a classic. First released in 1939, it has endured for generations. This paper examines three elements that contribute to its success: It uses the classic journey theme, has an archetypical hero character, and involves a battle of good and evil.

Journey themes have been used throughout literature. Joseph

Campbell describes this as the mythical journey. Here, the hero travels from home, goes to a foreign land, fights evil, attains new power, and returns home stronger then when the hero left. In the Wizard of Oz, Dorothy leaves Kansas and travels to another dimension. In this dimension she encounters evil in the form of the Wicked Witch of the West. Her new powers are her ruby red slippers. When she returns to Kansas, she has new insight that will supposedly help her become a better human and live a happier life.

In this movie, Dorothy is the archetypical hero figure used throughout literature and mythology. Like Luke Skywalker, Buddha, Galgamesh, Moses, and Jesus, there are questions regarding her parents. Why is she living with her aunt and uncle? What happened to Mr. and Mrs. Gale? Also, like most classical heroes, Dorothy has loyal companions who help her fight evil. Finally, Dorothy is the only character in the Oz movie to take a moral stance. When Lion first appears, he begins chasing Toto around the tree. Not knowing he was cowardly, Dorothy risked her life by slapping Lion on the nose. She tells him it is wrong for those who are bigger and stronger to pick on the small and the weak.

The concept of evil is very clearly defined in this movie. Here, the Wicked Witch of the West clearly illustrates what Jung would describe as our shadow or dark side. This is the part of our psyche, little explored, that houses our more base instincts. Much like the Satan figure in Christian mythologies and despots throughout history, the Witch projects this shadow side by her need to conquer and control. Dorothy, however, is clearly good and might be considered a projection of our higher nature.

Now, notice the difference when I take the same blob of text, insert some headings, and stick a cute little introductory paragraph on the front.

The Wizard of Oz

The Wizard of Oz is considered a classic. First released in 1939, it has endured for generations. This paper examines three elements that contribute to its success: (a) the use of the classic journey theme, (b) the archetypical hero character, and (c) the theme of good versus evil.

Journey Theme

Journey themes have been used throughout literature. Joseph Campbell describes this as the mythical journey. Here, the hero travels from home, goes to a foreign land, fights evil, attains new power, and returns home stronger then when the hero left. In the Wizard of Oz, Dorothy leaves Kansas and travels to another dimension. In this dimension she encounters evil in the form of the Wicked Witch of the West. Her new powers are her ruby red slippers. When she returns to Kansas, she has new insight that will supposedly help her become a better human and live a happier life.

Archetypical Hero

In this movie, Dorothy is the archetypical hero figure used throughout literature and mythology. Like Luke Skywalker, Buddha, Galgamesh, Moses, and Jesus, there are questions regarding her parents. Why is she living with her aunt and uncle? What happened to Mr. and Mrs. Gale? Also, like most classical heroes, Dorothy has loyal companions who help her fight evil. Finally, Dorothy is the only character in the Oz movie to take a moral stance. When Lion first appears, he begins chasing Toto around the tree. Not knowing he was cowardly, Dorothy risked her life by slapping Lion on the nose. She tells him it is wrong for those who are bigger and stronger to pick on the small and the weak.
Good and Evil
The concept of evil is very prevalent in this movie. Here, the Wicked Witch of the West clearly illustrates what Jung would describe as our shadow or dark side. This is the part of our psyche, little explored, that houses our more base instincts. Much like the Satan figure in Christian mythologies and despots throughout history, the Witch projects this shadow side by her need to conquer and control. Dorothy, however, is clearly good and might be considered a projection of our higher nature.

Introductory Paragraph.
A short introductory paragraph at the beginning gives the reader a preview and provides a sense of structure. This introductory paragraph is usually no more than three sentences. The last sentence of this paragraph uses some form of seriation to indicate the sections of the paper. (Seriation and the introductory paragraph will be explained in detail in the next section of this book.) Each of the ideas in the last sentence is used to create a heading for each section of the paper. The advantage of headings is that they create a visual sense of organization and help the reader transition from one section to another.
Subheadings
Subheadings help to organize a section. If I head a great deal of information under *Good and Evil* in the writing above, I would break this information up with subheadings. Subheadings are italicized, flush left, with the first letter of the principle words capitalized. Example:

Good and Evil
The concept of evil is very prevalent in this movie. Here, the Wicked Witch of the West clearly illustrates what Jung would describe as our shadow or dark side.
The Shadow Side
This is the part of our psyche, little explored, that houses our more base instincts. Much like the Satan figure in Christian mythologies and despots throughout history, the Witch projects this shadow side by her need to conquer and control. Dorothy, however, is clearly good and might

be considered a projection of our higher nature.

An Elusive Concept

Good and evil are not always easily defined. For example, in Kansas Toto bit Miss Gultch. This is not a good thing, and Miss Gultch was operating within the law in seeking to have Toto destroyed. Dorothy, on the other hand, allowed her dog to wander unattended. Also, she tried to run away from home without considering her family, she stole shoes that were not her own, she killed two witches, and ate apples that did not belong to her.

Chapter 12

Less is More

Communication being equal, fewer words are always preferable to more words. Using a few words makes your ideas more visible and more likely to be attended to. Using a great many words can camouflage your words and make it less likely that people will read your paper.

Section Three
The Particulars of Academic Writing

Chapter 13

The Introductory Paragraph

As described previously, the introductory paragraph is usually two to three sentences long. It should be just enough to give the reader a sense of what the paper is about and describe the specific points to be discussed. An example of this is the introductory paragraph for the Wizard of Oz piece in Chapter 11:

The Wizard of Oz
The Wizard of Oz is considered a classic. First released in 1939, it has endured for generations. This paper examines three elements that contribute to its success: (a) the use of the classic journey theme, (b) the archetypical hero character, and (c) the theme of good versus evil.

Here, the first two sentences are used to set the stage. At this point, the reader has a good idea of what the paper is about. The last sentence in the introductory paragraph uses some type of seriation (described below) to delineate the structure which is to follow. There are three benefits to using this type of seriated sentence in your introductory paragraph: (a) having a sense of the structure, the reader is able to see how the parts are related to the whole and thus, comprehension is increased, (b) it helps to create a smooth transition between sections, and (c) it forces you to find and use structure in your writing.

Seriation
Seriation, a word that will not appear on most spell checkers, means organizing things in a series. Mastering the subtle art of seriation will enhance both your thinking and writing. Below seriation is described using (a) commas; (b) letters and commas; (c) a colon, letters, and commas; (d) a semicolon, colon, letters, and commas, and (e) a colon, numbers, and paragraphs.

Commas Only
When you have three or more things in a list, use the comma to separate them.

Example: People become better writers by reading good writing, listening to others who speak well, writing as much and as often as possible, and getting feedback on their writing.

Some sources say that a comma should not be used before 'and' in a seriated sentence.

Example A: Apples, oranges and banana.

Others say that 'and' is treated like any other item in a seriated sentence.

Example B: Apples, oranges, and bananas.

Both are technically correct; however, for academic writing, Example B is the one that should be used.

Letters and Commas

When listing three or more things in a series, use letters (not numbers) inside of parentheses to separate the ideas. (Make sure your parentheses are 2-sided.) This type of seriation is very visual and makes it much easier for the reader comprehend.

Example: People become better writers by (a) reading good writing, (b) listening to others who speak well, (c) writing as much and as often as possible, and (d) getting feedback on their writing.

Colon, Letters, and Commas

Use a colon when what follows extends or amplifies the preceding material.

Example: People become better writers by: (a) reading good writing, (b) listening to others who speak well, (c) writing as much and as often as possible, and (d) getting feedback on their writing.

If the information that follows the colon is a complete sentence, start this with a capital letter.

Example: People become better writers by engaging in various activities: They can (a) read good writing, (b) listen to others who speak well, (c) write as much and as often as possible, and (d) get plenty of feedback on their writing.

Semi-Colon, Colon, Letters, and Commas

When a series of items, ideas, or sentences has internal commas, use a semicolon to separate the items, ideas, or sentences.

Example A: There are four things people can do to become better writers: read many books, magazines, and journal articles; listen and pay attention to word usage in lectures, conversations, and speeches; write as much and as often as possible; and get feedback on their writing from friends, roommates, and classmates.

Example B: There are four things people can do to become better writers: (a) read many books, magazines, and journal articles; (b) listen and pay attention to word usage in lectures, conversations, and speeches; (c) write as much and as often as possible; and (d) get feedback on their writing from friends, roommates, and classmates.

Both the examples above are correct. Without the semicolon, it would be very hard to separate the items, ideas, or sentences.

Colon, Numbers, and Paragraphs

When each successive item or point becomes a paragraph, indent and use numbers to delineate each point. The numeral symbol takes the place of the number words: 'first', 'second', 'third', etc.

Example: There are four things people can do to become better writers:

1. Read good writing. This will help beginning writers begin to perceive the form, structure, and style that other writers use; develop vocabulary; and help to cultivate an internal sense of grammar.

2. Listen to others who speak well. This will help to develop vocabulary as well as provide models related to the form and structure of sentences.

3. Write as much and as often as possible. Organizing ideas, putting them together on paper, and revising is the fastest and most efficient way to develop writing skills. People cannot expect to become better writers without a good deal of writing practice.

4. Get feedback. Getting feedback on writing assignments gives beginning writers a sense of audience. Here, they are able to see how the writing plays inside the head of a reader. Also, other people are often able to help generate ideas that might not have been considered.

Do Not Become Seriation Happy

Do not overuse this technique. Below is an example of bad seriation:

The Wizard of Oz

The Wizard of Oz is considered a classic movie. First released in

1939, it has endured for generations. This paper examines three elements that contribute to its success: it (a) uses the classic journey theme, (b) has an archetypical hero character, and (c) involves a battle of good and evil.

Journey Theme

Journey themes, as described by Joseph Campbell, have been used throughout literature and contain four main ideas: (a) the hero travels from home, goes to a foreign land, fights evil, attains new power, and returns home stronger then when the hero left; (b) the hero attains new strength, wisdom, or powers; (c) there is an encounter and a struggle against evil; and (d) the hero returns home a better and more powerful human.

Traveling From Home

Heros might travel from home in various ways or for various reasons: (a) in search of adventure, (b) on a religious quest, (c) by accident, or (d) against their will.

Because seriation in the form of letters and parentheses is used in the introductory paragraph above, it gets very cumbersome if it is used immediately in the subsequent section. Likewise, if it is used after the heading it gets very cumbersome if used immediately in the subheading. If seriation is overused, your paper will begin to sound like a series of lists.

Chapter 14

Paragraphs

Paragraphs are a group of sentences organized around an idea. They create a physical break between one idea and the next. Paragraphs also help writers organize their thinking and help the reader perceive the structure of the writing. Without paragraphs the writing becomes simply of glob of text that can be very hard to read. Below is an example of an unpublished manuscript without paragraphs:

B.F. Skinner was a psychologist who applied behaviorism to studying learning. While Pavlov used stimuli to produce certain responses (using a bell to get a dog to salivate), Skinner used the consequences which followed responses to shape behavior. Using consequences or reinforcers to shape behavior is known as operant conditioning. This article describes what choir directors might learn from B.F. Skinner and dancing chickens. A reinforcer is any consequence that increases the frequency of a behavior. Conditioning is the parceling out of reinforcement. Through conditioning, behaviors are gradually shaped. In a choir there are certain behaviors that will enhance learning and help to produce a better vocal sound. Define the desired behaviors and begin to consider the forces to be used in shaping current behaviors in the desired direction. Behaviors that are rewarded are more likely to be repeated. For singers, one type of reward or positive reinforcement is recognition or praise by the director. When a particular passage is sung well, it should be noticed and reinforced. When the choir sings with feeling or a particular technique is done well, the director should respond to it. You do not have to stop the song to deliver these reinforcers. "Nice job tenors," is a little Skinnerian pellet that is easy to deliver. Also, in analyzing behaviors consider the motive behind each behavior. Why do your singers want to sing? Why did they join the choir? Why do they keep coming back? For most, the act of making music and singing is pleasurable. They enjoy creating harmonies, producing beautiful sounds, and performing. Each of these can become a positive reinforcer. Music that is within the difficulty range of the singers can be learned and those pleasurable aesthetic qualities can be enjoyed. Music that is too difficult becomes a technical event rather than a musical event and can overwhelm and frustrate singers. Instead of a positive reinforcer, it can become an aversive conditioner and have the opposite effect. The social aspects of choirs can also be a positive reinforcer that keeps singers coming back. This is especially true for junior high and high school choirs.

Allowing five minutes for singers to talk at the end of a rehearsal is not wasted time. Also, frequently mixing up the voices so singers get a chance to interact cannot only help musically, but can enhance the social and interpersonal elements of your choir. Behaviors that are not rewarded are less likely to be repeated. When a productive behavior is followed by no reinforcement (no attention or recognition), that behavior is less likely to be repeated. Noticing productive behaviors is important in shaping a choir. If a desired behavior has been identified, such as breath control, support, a particular tone quality, or a feeling on some musical passages, teach it explicitly, then reinforce as it occurs ...

Just looking at the large blob of text is enough to scare most readers away. Notice how the inclusion of paragraphs below breaks up the text and separates the ideas.

B.F. Skinner was a psychologist who applied behaviorism to studying learning. While Pavlov used stimuli to produce certain responses (using a bell to get a dog to salivate), Skinner used the consequences which followed responses to shape behavior. Using consequences or reinforcers to shape behavior is known as operant conditioning. This article describes what choir directors might learn from B.F. Skinner and dancing chickens.

A reinforcer is any consequence that increases the frequency of a behavior. Conditioning is the parceling out of reinforcement. Through conditioning, behaviors are gradually shaped. In a choir there are certain behaviors that will enhance learning and help to produce a better vocal sound. Define the desired behaviors and begin to consider the forces to be used in shaping current behaviors in the desired direction.

Behaviors that are rewarded are more likely to be repeated. For singers, one type of reward or positive reinforcement is recognition or praise by the director. When a particular passage is sung well, it should be noticed and reinforced. When the choir sings with feeling or a particular technique is done well, the director should respond to it. You do not have to stop the song to deliver these reinforcers. "Nice job tenors," is a little Skinnerian pellet that is easy to deliver.

Also, in analyzing behaviors consider the motive behind each behavior. Why do your singers want to sing? Why did they join the choir? Why do they keep coming back? For most, the act of making music and singing is pleasurable. They enjoy creating harmonies, producing beautiful sounds, and performing. Each of these can become a positive reinforcer. Music that is within the difficulty range of the singers can be learned and those pleasurable aesthetic qualities can be enjoyed. Music that is too difficult becomes a technical event rather than a musical event and can overwhelm and frustrate singers. Instead of a positive reinforcer, it can become an aversive conditioner and have the opposite effect.

The social aspects of choirs can also be a positive reinforcer that keeps singers coming back. This is especially true for junior high and high school choirs. Allowing five minutes for singers to talk at the end of a rehearsal is not wasted time. Also, frequently mixing up the voices so singers get a chance to interact cannot only help musically, but can enhance the social and interpersonal elements of your choir.

Behaviors that are not rewarded are less likely to be repeated. When a productive behavior is followed by no reinforcement (no attention or recognition), that behavior is less likely to be repeated. Noticing productive behaviors is important in shaping a choir. If a desired behavior has been identified, such as breath control or a particular tone quality, teach it explicitly, then reinforce it as it occurs ...

The inclusion of a title, headings, and subheadings creates even more structure.

Using Behaviorism in High School Choirs

B.F. Skinner was a psychologist who applied behaviorism to studying learning. While Pavlov used stimuli to produce certain responses (using a bell to get a dog to salivate), Skinner used the consequences which followed responses to shape behavior. Using consequences or reinforcers to shape behavior is known as operant conditioning. This article describes what choir directors might learn from B.F. Skinner and dancing chickens.

Operant Conditioning

A reinforcer is any consequence that increases the frequency of a behavior. Conditioning is the parceling out of reinforcement. Through conditioning, behaviors are gradually shaped. In a choir there are certain behaviors that will enhance learning and help to produce a better vocal sound. Define the desired behaviors and begin to consider the forces to be used in shaping current behaviors in the desired direction.

Positive Reinforcement or Rewards

Behaviors that are rewarded are more likely to be repeated. For singers, one type of reward or positive reinforcement is recognition or praise by the director. When a particular passage is sung well, it should be noticed and reinforced. When the choir sings with feeling or a particular technique is done well, the director should respond to it. You do not have to stop the song to deliver these reinforcers. "Nice job tenors," is a little Skinnerian pellet that is easy to deliver.

Aesthetic Reinforcers

In analyzing behaviors, consider the motive behind each behavior. Why do your singers want to sing? Why did they join the choir? Why do they keep coming back? For most, the act of making music and singing is pleasurable. Singers enjoy creating harmonies, producing beautiful sounds, and performing. Each of these can become a positive reinforcer. Music that is within the difficulty range of the singers can be learned and the pleasurable aesthetic qualities can be enjoyed. Music that is too difficult becomes a technical event rather than a musical event and can overwhelm and frustrate singers. Instead of a positive reinforcer, it can become an aversive conditioner and have the opposite effect.

Social Reinforcers

The social aspects of choirs can also be a positive reinforcer that keeps singers coming back. This is especially true for junior high and high school choirs. Allowing five minutes for singers to talk at the end of a rehearsal is not wasted time. Also, frequently mixing up the voices so singers get a chance to interact cannot only help musically, but can enhance the social and interpersonal elements of your choir.

Extinction or Non Reinforcement

Behaviors that are not rewarded are less likely to be repeated. When a productive behavior is followed by no reinforcement (no attention or recognition), that behavior is less likely to be repeated. Noticing productive behaviors is important in shaping a choir. If a desired behavior has been identified, such as breath control or a particular tone quality, teach it explicitly, then reinforce it as it occurs ...

New Paragraphs

A paragraph should have unity, a theme, focus, or a central idea. Start a new paragraph when you feel yourself wandering into a new idea. When in doubt, create a new paragraph; however, avoid one-sentence paragraphs.

Topics and Topic Sentences

Traditionally it was taught that every paragraph had to have a topic sentence; however, this is not always true. It may be easier to think of every paragraph as having a topic or theme. That is, you identify one main idea, say it, and then use the rest of the paragraph to support or explain that idea. Below, I wanted to say that the flying monkeys in the *Wizard of Oz* were really midgets in monkey suits. This is the topic of the paragraph. The other sentences support or elaborate this idea. When I found myself wandering off onto something else, I started a new paragraph.

The flying monkeys in the movie, *The Wizard of Oz* were not real. That is, they were not real monkeys and they could not fly. They were midgets in monkey suits. If you look closely, you can see the zipper on the back of their suits. Also, in the scene where the flying monkeys fly in and pick up Dorothy and Toto, you can see the wire they travel down.

This is all part of the magic of movies. The movie *Mary Poppins* has a scene where Bert, Mary Poppins, and the children go for tea and begin to laugh. As they laugh, they find themselves beginning to float up into the air. Soon the entire tea party is laughing and giggling on the ceiling of the room. However, like monkeys, people cannot fly or float in the air. This was an illusion accomplished with wires and head shots.

The first paragraph above was my flying monkey paragraph. The second was my Mary Poppins paragraph. Below, I have broken up one idea (time), into two parts. When I began to explain the second part, I created a new paragraph. In this way the delineation between the two ideas becomes very visual.

The ancient Chinese had two ideas related to time: First, Lou-shou, which is what we commonly think of as linear time. This view conceives of time as a straight, unending progression of dominos falling from past, to present, to future. The universe is a series of causes and effects. One thing happens, which in turn causes another, and another, and another, and so on.
The second view of time is Hou-tou, which is circular time. Here, time is perceived as a puddle where the past, present, and future all touch each other. This view does not see the universe as a series of cause and effects, rather, things happen in fields where like things attract each other. This is the time found in the Universal Unconscious. Here, we are touched simultaneously by Christmas past and Christmas yet-to-be. In Hou-tou, sometimes the effect comes before the cause.

It is helpful to the reader if the main ideas or themes of your paragraph are stated first. This can help make your paragraphs easier to read, which is the ultimate goal. Do not make the reader wade through most of your paragraph to discover your point. Remember that a confused or frustrated reader soon becomes a non reader.

Conceptual Leaps
A conceptual leap is where the writer suddenly leaps from one thing to another, leaving the reader struggling to find the bridge between the two. Conceptual leaps within paragraphs and between paragraphs are to be avoided.

Less effective: Movies and dreams are very similar. Movies might even be thought of as a public dream. The film-watching state, with its relaxed posture and slowed breathing, represents a form of sleep. Both are illusions. Dreams are very much like prophecies. Science fiction is an important imaginative type of dream. Things have to be thought of before they can come into being.
The paragraph above contains some interesting ideas; however, instead of developing and supporting them, the writer jumps from one idea to the next. Below, the writer develops each idea and makes a smooth transition from movies to dreams to science fiction. The topic of dreams

is the unifying element here.

More effective: Dreams and movies are very similar. Movies might be thought of as a public dream. With both, the observer is sitting in a passive state in a dark room. Both are illusions that rely on images. However, in the film-watching state, things are more logical and observers know they are watching a move. In dreams, things tend to be scattered and disjointed, and observers do not always know they are dreaming.

Dreams are also very much like prophecies. Both are illusions that rely on metaphors that must be personally interpreted. To try to attend to either of them literally is to miss the point. Their power comes from allowing the subjective mind to project onto them.

Science fiction might be a form of an imaginative dream. Science fiction is dreaming about or projecting into the future, a future which is an illusion.

Above, the writer develops each idea. In paragraphs two and three, the first sentence provides a transition from one paragraph to the next. The main idea or theme is stated first while the remaining sentences are used to support, explore, or elaborate this idea.

Paragraph Length

How long should paragraphs be? Long enough to develop the point or idea. Short enough to prevent the reader from being bored or confused. More complicated ideas require larger paragraphs; less complicated ideas require smaller paragraphs.

Redundancy Within the Paragraph

Generally, say things only once in a paragraph. Repeating an idea clutters up your writing and adds to the confusion.

Less effective: What you do before you begin writing is just as important as what you doing during writing. The goal of the prewriting activity is to gather information and generate ideas. A prewriting activity actually makes writing easier. The prewriting activity is a critical part of the writing process.

The writer above wanted to stress that prewriting activities are important, however, restating the same idea does little to make the original idea a better one.

More effective: The prewriting activity is a critical part of the writing process. The goal here is to gather information and generate ideas. Prewriting activities actually make writing easier.

Redundancy Within the Paper

Finally, avoid redundancy within your paper. If you have stated an idea in another place, you may refer to it, but it should not be presented as something new. Again, the reader does not know if you are introducing a new idea, or somehow they misread a similar idea when it was first stated. (Notice how simply including the word "again" in the previous sentence lets the reader know that this idea had appeared before. This is the proper way to repeat things. Other phrases to use here include, "as stated previously," "once again," "to reiterate," or "to repeat.")

Chapter 15

Transition Words and Sentences

The onus is always on you to make clear connections between one thing and the next. Good academic writing reads like melted butter: It flows smoothly. Transition words and sentences are two techniques to create this melted butter affect.

Transition Words

Transition words provide a variety of cues for the reader. Below are eight categories and related transition words (Meriwether, 1996):

Argument or concession: admittedly, certainly, consequently, furthermore, in fact, of course, undoubtedly.

Cause and effect: accordingly, because, since, thereafter, thus, whereas.

Condition: even though, if, in case, nevertheless, on condition that, therefore.

Connectives: additionally, after, again, also, and, as well as, before, besides, formerly, finally, further, in addition, last, later, next, previously, since, then, too.

Differences: although, but, even so, however, on the contrary, otherwise.

Similarities: as, like, likewise, resemble, similar to, just as.

Example: for example, for instance, thus, to illustrate.

Summary: finally, in conclusion, therefore, thus, to sum up.

Transition Sentences

Just as conceptual leaps within paragraphs are to be avoided, so too are conceptual leaps between paragraphs as they leave the reader confused and disrupt comprehension. Transition sentences at the end or beginning of paragraphs create a more unified and coherent piece. This is illustrated in the piece below where the transition sentences are in bold face.

Reality

If you look deep enough, you see that there is no difference between reality and fantasy, between this and that, here and there, subjective and objective, the idea and the thing. All are variants of the same reality. All are waves; temporary forms consisting of the same water. **Thich Nhat Hanh (1999), the Buddhist mystic, describes two levels of reality that exist simultaneously:** *Phenomenal reality* is the reality of things seen, that which we are used to seeing and experiencing. These are the waves, bits of reality coming into temporary form. This reflects the objective outer world where truth is determined by repeatability and the laws of cause and effect. Noumenal reality is the reality inaccessible to logic or the normal senses. This is the water, the essence of all things, the ground of all being, God, Allah, Jehovah, WaTonka, Brahman, Oz. This reflects the subjective inner world where truth is determined by meaning.

Plato used the allegory of a cave to explain these two dimensions of reality. According to the allegory, we live inside a cave. Those things that appear in the physical world as real to us (phenomenal reality), are only shadows on the wall of this cave caused by the sun shining on the true things outside (noumenal reality). Everything inside the cave is temporary.

You may look at the chair you're sitting on and say, *"Wait a minute, how can this be? This chair is not temporary. It's right here and I'm sitting on it."* But even as you sit, that chair is in a state of decay. Someday the chair as you know it will be like the wave that has crashed upon the shore. Its form will be dissipated and its parts scattered. **Thus, the chair is real, but a very temporary manifestation.**

More permanent manifestations reside outside the cave. Here, the outer is the inner. This is the subjective world of invisible ideas where the sun shines. Noumenal reality is the realm where the authenticity of phenomena is determined by connotation or what it suggests, rather than denotation or what attributes it consists of. Consequently, those images that appear to us here are absolutely real and authentic insofar as we can determine their meanings.

The very transitory nature of what we call the physical realm and its relation to time is described aptly by Stephen Hawkings (1988) in, *A Brief History of Time*. Think of a puddle of milk spilled on a table top and spreading outward as the beginning of what we know as phenomenal reality. However, instead of two dimensions, think of it expanding in three dimensions like a balloon. As this puddle expands outward it becomes thinner. Thus, we are essentially fading away like the Cheshire cat. Hawkings posits that reality as we know it is moving from perfect order (the pre-spilt-milk-condition) to chaos (spilt-milk and beyond).

So in terms of inner or outer; subject or objective, one is no more real than the other; however, one is more permanent. Thus, Plato, Buddha, St. Paul, and Jesus all stressed ideas or ideals such as personal virtues, consciousness, compassion, understanding, consciousness, and harmonious relations among the facilities of the soul, for these are eternal things.

References

Hawkings, S. W. (1988). *A brief history of time: From big bang to black holes.* New York: Bantom Books.

Meriwether, N.W. (1996). *Twelve easy steps to successful research papers*. Lincolnwood, IL: NTC Publishing Group.

Nhat Hanh, T. (1999). *Going home: Jesus and Buddha as brothers*. New York: Riverhead Books.

Chapter 16

Grammar and Punctuation

Grammar

Grammar is the study of the way language works, a description of the structure of our language. Correct grammar usage helps to create precision in writing and speaking. While you do not have to be a grammarian to write well, you do have to learn a few basic grammar rules and develop an intuitive sound for the language. This chapter describes seven grammar tips and a couple of punctuation tidbits that should get you through most academic writing situations.

There are two ways to check your writing for grammar errors: First, have other people read your work. Second, use the grammar check programs that come with most word processor programs. While not always reliable, grammar checks can find many grammar mistakes, and they provide you with short grammar lessons as you use them.

Avoiding the Seven Most Common Grammar Errors

1. Stay consistent with tense. You may not switch tense on a whim. If you use the past tense in the first part of a sentence or paragraph, you must use it throughout.

Incorrect: After John hit the ball he ran. He stumbles on the way to first (past tense and present tense).

Correct: After John hit the ball he ran. He stumbled on the way to first (both use past tense).

Correct: John hits the ball and runs. He stumbles on the way to first base (both use present tense).

Incorrect: The accident happened because people drive too fast (past and present tense).

Correct: The accident happened because people were driving too fast (past tense).

Correct: Accidents happen because people drive too fast (present tense).

Incorrect: Bill is dirty because he was (past) out working and his dog keeps (present) knocking him down.

Correct: Bill is dirty because his dog keeps knocking him down when he is working.

Correct: Bill is dirty because he was out working and his dog kept knocking him down.

2. Stay consistent with plurality. You also may not switch plurality on a whim. If you use the singular in the first part of a sentence or paragraph, you must use it throughout.

Incorrect: A person (singular) should always have their (plural) notebooks.
Correct: A person should always have a notebook.
Correct: People should always have their notebooks.

Incorrect: The class (singular) improved their (plural) scores 30%.
Correct: The class improved its score by 30%.
Correct: People in the class improved their scores by 30%.

Incorrect: A dog (singular) should be allowed to remove their (plural) collars.
Correct: Dogs should be allowed to remove their collars.
Correct: A dog should be allowed to remove its collars.

Incorrect: A child (singular) often worries about their (plural) first day of school.
Correct: Children often worry about their first day of school.
Correct: A child often worries about the first day of school.

3. Double pronouns should make sense when one is missing. This means that if you read the sentence with just one of either pronouns, that sentence should still make sense.

Incorrect: Me and her will go to the dance. (Me will go to the dance. Her will go to the dance.)
Correct: She and I will go to the dance. (She will go to the dance. I will go to the dance.)

Incorrect: Kelli and her discussed the plan. (Kelli discussed the plan. Her discussed the plan.)
Correct: Kelli and she discussed the plan. (Kelli discussed the plan. She discussed the plan.)

Incorrect: The prize went to he and I. (The prize went to he. The prize went to I.)
Correct: The prize went to him and me. (The prize went to him. The prize went to me.)

Incorrect: Him and me went to the movie. (Him went to the movie. Me went to the movie.)
Incorrect: Him and I went to the movie. (Him went to the movie. I went to the movie.)
Correct: He and I went to the movie. (He went to the movie. I went to the movie.)

4. Stay gender neutral.

Incorrect: Every person has to make his own decision.
Correct: Every person has to make his or her own decision.
Best: People have to make their own decisions.

Incorrect: Firemen work long and hard.
Correct: Firefighters work long and hard.

Incorrect: This lake is manmade.
Correct: This lake is made by humans.
Correct: This lake is human made.

5. Avoid repetition within a sentence. By striving trying to use as few words as possible you will avoid most problems with repetition and redundancy.

Incorrect: Steve often comes to school tired so we must try to get Steve to bed on time.
Correct: Steve often comes to school tired. We must try to get him to bed on time.
Correct: Steve often comes to school tired, therefore, we must try to get him to bed on time.

6. Use 'that' for restrictive clauses and 'which' for nonrestrictive clauses. A restrictive clause is one in which the clause or point is essential to the meaning of the sentence. Use 'that' in these instances.

Example: The class that used Andy's book produced excellent writers.

The sentence above indicates that there was a class that used Andy's book and there was also at least one other class that did not. The class that used Andy's book produced excellent writers. Thus, the clause is essential to the point of the sentence as we are clearly identifying a particular class.
A nonrestrictive clause is like a theatrical aside. It adds dimension to

the idea, however, the meaning is still largely intact if the clause were not there. Use 'which' in these instances.

Example: The class, *which used Andy's book,* produced excellent writers.

In the sentence above, the main idea is that the class produced excellent writers. They just happened to have used Andy's book. It does not indicate that there was another class.

7. *Use 'that' for restrictive clauses and 'who' for nonrestrictive clauses.*

Restrictive clause: Those students that are done with their work may go to recess.
Nonrestrictive clause: Those students, who are done with their work, may go to recess.

The first one indicates that only those students finished with their work are to be allowed to go recess. The second one indicates that these students are allowed to go to recess and also, they just happen to be done with their work.

Punctuation

This section describes the punctuation information you will need to get you through the majority of your writing projects.

The Comma

A comma is used in the following situations:

1. Between elements. Use a comma to separate items in a series. A comma should be used before the last 'and' or 'or' in the sentence.

Incorrect: The apples oranges and bananas fell to the ground.
Incorrect: The apples, oranges and bananas fell to the ground.
Correct: The apples, oranges, and bananas fell to the ground.

2. To separate a nonessential clause. A nonessential clause, like the nonrestrictive clause described above, is like a theatrical aside. Here, the message is still intact without its inclusion.

Nonessential clause: The orange, which had been handled by George, fell to the ground.

The sentence above indicates that an orange fell to the floor and it just happened to have been handled by George. This is an example of a nonessential clause. The George part of the sentence is an interesting but not essential part of this sentence.

An essential clause means that the information in the middle of the sentence is vital to the stuff at the end and should not be separated by a comma. In the sentence below, there was more than one orange, but only the one handled by George fell to the floor. This is an essential clause, thus *'that'* is used instead of *'which'*.

Essential clause: The orange that had been handled by George fell to the floor.

3. To separate two independent clauses joined by a conjunction. If you have a compound sentence where both sides of the sentence would be complete sentences by themselves, use a comma.

Two independent clauses: Apples are better than oranges, and bananas are often used for pie.

Both parts of this sentence above would work as sentences by themselves: Apples are better than oranges. Bananas are often used for pie. A comma is used here to separate them. In the sentence below, a comma is not used. "Apples are better than oranges" is a complete sentence, however, 'they are often used for pie' depends on the first part of the sentence for it to make sense, thus, it is a dependent clause.

A compound sentence with one dependent clause: Apples are better than oranges and they are often used for pie.

Do not use a comma to separate two parts of a compound sentence.

Incorrect: Margaret Hamilton played the Wicked Witch, and later starred in coffee commercials.
Correct: Margaret Hamilton played the Wicked Witch and later starred in coffee commercials.

The Semicolon

A semicolon is used in the following situations:

1. To separate two independent clauses that are not joined by a conjunction. This means the semicolon takes the place of *and, but*, and *or*.

No semicolon: The winners were happy but the losers were sad.
Semicolon: The winners were happy; the losers were sad.

2. To separate elements in a series that already contain commas. If I wanted to list a series of things in different groups (some fruit things, some vegetable things, and some dairy things), I would use the commas to separate the things within the groups and semicolons to separate the groups. This way the reader knows when the groups end and begin.

Incorrect: For breakfast there was apples, oranges, and pears, carrots, peas, and beans, and yogurt, cottage cheese, and milk.
Correct: For breakfast there was apples, oranges, and pears; carrots, peas, and beans; and yogurt, cottage cheese, and milk.

The Colon
The rule of thumb for the colon is that everything that follows the colon should directly relate to what preceded it. This is done two ways:
1. A complete introductory clause followed by a final clause to illustrate the point.

Example: There were three kinds of fruit: apples, oranges, and pears.

2. A complete introductory clause followed by a complete sentence that illustrates the point.

Example: All three agree: Fruit is best for breakfast.

The illustrating sentence that follows the colon above is a complete sentence; thus, it begins with a capital letter.

Final Thoughts
The information included above should get you through most writing situations. I would suggest you put a post-it note here, as you will be referring back here quite often. If you have any further questions, I would refer you to the Publication Manual of the American Psychological Association (2001).

References
American Psychological Association (2001). *Publication manual of the American Psychological Association* (5th ed.). Washington, DC.

Chapter 17

Sentences

Long Sentences

Sentences that are too long will confuse the reader and make your writing less powerful. Remember, short term memory has a limited capacity and can hold only about 7 chunks of information for about 15 seconds.

Less effective: Despite the importance of writing in high school and college and the need to write effectively in the business and professional world, students seem not to realize the necessity of learning the process of writing, which is essential in creating powerful writing, even though this process is enhanced greatly by computers and word processing programs.

With a sentence this long, the reader has to try to hold onto the ideas at the beginning of the sentence while processing those found at the end. This clutters STM and creates anger and confusion.

Short Sentences

If you rely exclusively on short sentences, your writing will sound choppy and disjointed.

Less effective: Writing is important in high school and college. People in the business and professional world also need to write effectively. It is important to learn the process of writing. Students do not seem to realize this. Knowing the process of writing is essential in creating powerful writing. The writing process is enhanced greatly by computers and word processing programs.

Long and Short Sentences

It is best to mix the length of your sentences.

More effective: Being able to write effectively is important in high school and college as well as in the business and professional world. Learning the process of writing will help you create powerful writing. Computers can be used to this end.

Chapter 18

Citations

Citing sources supports your ideas and sets them in a theoretical context. Citations also allow readers to find your supporting documents, they acknowledge the authors, and they make your writing more credible. Citing is different from quoting, which will be described in the next chapter. When citing, you must paraphrase the author's ideas.

Citing in the Text

This section describes how to cite various types of material in the body of your work.

One Author - One Article

You wish to cite a study or an article written by Johnson without quoting him:

A recent study found that those college students who used an objective stance in their writing earned significantly higher salaries after college than college students who used a subjective stance in their writing (Johnson, 1995).

Instead of citing a particular study, you may wish to cite a published author to lend credibility to what you have to say.

In academic writing, the writer generally tries to use an objective, academic voice (Johnson, 1995).

More than One Author - One Article

Use a comma to separate the authors and the "&" symbol instead of the word 'and' inside the parentheses.

A recent study found that the freshmen composition papers that received the highest grades used an objective, academic voice (Johnson, Smith, & Varnum, 1995).

More than One Article

If many authors reach the same point, you will need to cite more than one article or study. In the sentence below all those authors cited at the end of the sentence found that writing shapes thinking. Within the parenthesis, the authors are put in alphabetical order. A semicolon is used to separate them.

Studies have found that writing shapes thinking (Anderson, 1995; Johnson, 1995; Marx, H. 1996).

In the sample below, I used the piling-on technique. Here, I found many authors who wrote articles and books that recommended using an objective voice with academic writing.

Academic writing is most persuasive if the writing uses logic and an objective, academic voice (Abbot, 1995; Costello, 1999; Fife & Taylor, 1998; Hardy & Laurel, 1987; Keaton & Marx, 1999; Wartbuam, 1995; Zemmelman, 1998).

Three or More Authors for One Article
Sometimes articles are written by three or more authors. Here the citation ends up sounding like a law firm. The first time you cite this in the text you must list all the authors with a comma between the last names.

A recent study found that too much milk makes breakfast cereal soggy (Howard, Fine, & Howard, 1987).

Three or More Authors the Next Time
After you have made a full citation with three or more authors, you can use a shortcut with all subsequent citations by the same authors. Here you list the first author followed by, *et al.* and the year.

Most breakfast eaters report using more than one spoon of sugar on unsweetened breakfast cereal (Howard et al., 1987).

Citing by Mentioning the Author's Name
If you refer to the author of an article in your text, you simply need to put the year behind the name.

Keaton (1998) found that bananas are the fruit most often used with breakfast cereal.

If you mention an article written by two or more authors in your text, as opposed to citing within parenthesis, write the whole word 'and' instead of the symbol and also put the year behind the name.

Keaton and Arbuckle (1991) found that asparagus was seldom used with breakfast cereal.

A Word of Warning

A word of warning about the use of citations: Do not let other voices dominate your work.

Less effective: Barnes (1997) suggested that apple pies are dangerous. Trigby and Smith (1992) reported that the consumption of apple pie leads to delusional episodes. Hardy (1998) found that people who ingest apple pie are much more likely to smoke marijuana.

Instead of using words like *suggested, reported,* and *found*; simply state the idea in your own words and support it with a citation. This allows you to maintain a more powerful writing voice and makes it much easier to read.

More effective: Apple pies are dangerous (Barnes, 1997). Eating apple pie results in delusional episodes (Trigby & Smith, 1992) and can lead to marijuana smoking (Hardy 1998).

Say it and cite it. It is distracting to read a paper filled with things other people have said.

Less effective: Jones (1995) says that prewriting strategies are an important part of the writing process. Smith (1991) suggests that they may help to produce a more coherent paper. Gale (1989) found that using a prewriting strategy actually decreased the amount of time it took to write a paper. Bower (1994) recommends that prewriting strategies be used to cure writers' block.

The paragraph above contains some good ideas but they are hard to get to. I keep bumping into other people and this makes the writer seem like a timid little mouse.

In the paragraph below, fewer words are used, and the reader does not have to stumble over a department store full of people. It also creates a more authoritative voice.

More effective: Prewriting strategies are an important part of the writing process (Jones, 1995). They help to produce a more coherent paper (Smith, 1991), and decrease the amount of time spent writing (Gale, 1989). Also, prewriting strategies are one way to cure writers' block (Bower, 1994).

The Reference Page

The reference page contains the full reference citations of all articles that were cited in the body of the text. These are listed in alphabetical order by the author's last name. Everything cited or quoted in the body of your text must appear here. Also, you may not put any citations on the reference page that do not appear in the body of your text. Hanging citations are used on the reference page. That means the author and date are flush left. The next line of the citation and all that follows are indented five spaces. This section describes what the full reference citations should look like.

Journals, Magazines, and Newspapers

Journal Articles with One Author

A reference citation for a journal article contains the following: (a) the authors' last name, a comma, initials, comma, and a period; (b) year the article was published in parentheses followed by a period; (c) the name of the journal article capitalizing only the first letter and the letter of the word which appears directly after a colon, followed by a period; (d) the name of the journal, capital letters on the first letter of the major words, italicized, followed by a comma, (e) the volume number with a continued underline, followed by a comma; and (f) the pages upon which the article is found followed by a period.

Author, P. (2001). Name of the article. *Name of the Journal, 32,* 34-41.
McGovern, R. (1995). I can't believe it. *Liberal Digest, 3,* 123-129.

Journal Articles with a Colon in the Title

The first word in the title of a journal article that follows the colon is capitalized. There are no extra spaces between citations.

Johnson, A. (1997). The key to writing well: Buy my book. *The Journal of Writing, 57(4),* 234-301.
Laurel, S. (1992). The referenced page: Indenting is important. *Writing Today, 34,* 87-90.
Shakespear, W. (1999). Writing successfully: Reading a lot and revising often. *Writer's Quarterly, 57,* 34-55.

Journal Articles with More than One Author

Articles with more than one author are the same as above except that the authors' names and initials are separated with a comma.

Johnson, A., Finely, T., & Hanson, E. (1998). The magic of paragraphs. *The Brighton Journal of Writing, 57,* 122-131.

An Article Found in a Magazine

As discussed earlier, magazine articles are not the best sources to use in an academic article. Use them sparingly.

Johnson, A. (1994, July 16). Writing and thinking. *Newsweek*, 39-42.

A Newspaper Article

Newspaper articles are also not very good sources to use in academic writing. Be equally spare in their use.

Johnson, A. (1995, September 5). Writing well affects employment status of college grads. *The New York Times,* p. A11.

Books

Books With One Author

A reference citation from a book is similar to that of a journal article. It contains the following: (a) the authors last name, a comma, initials, comma, and a period; (b) year the book was published in parentheses followed by a period; (c) the name of the book italicized, capitalizing only the first letter, followed by a period; (d) the place in which is was published, and (e) the publisher.

Author, P. (1995). *Name of the book.* City, State: Publisher.
Johnson, A. (2003). *A short guide to academic writing.* Lanham, ML: University Press of America.

Books With a Colon in the Title

Just as with a journal article, the first letter of the first word directly following a full colon in the title is capitalized.

Johnson, A. (1999). *Writing a good term paper: Listening to what Andy has to say.* Needham, MA: Ellen & Bacon.

Books With Many Authors

Just as with journal articles, include a comma between the authors and use the symbol '&' instead of the word 'and'.

Johnson, A., Smith, T., Finely, T., & Mortenson, B. (1998). *The importance of listening to Andy.* Needham, MA: Ellen & Bacon.

Books of a Later Edition

A book published in 1999 may be the third or fourth editions of one written earlier. This tells the reader that the book was so popular that it was updated and later editions were printed. Here, *(4th ed.)* is in parentheses, *and 'ed'* is in lowercase with a period after it. A period also follows the last paren.

Johnson, A. (2008). *A short guide to action research* (4th ed.). Needham, MH: Allyn & Bacon.

An Edited Book

This means that one or more people have edited the writings of several different authors and put them in a book. This is identified by including *(Ed.)* for one editor or *(Eds.)* for more than one editor. *Ed* starts with a capital letter so that the reader is able to quickly make the distinction between edition and editor. In the first citation below, we can assume that editor Barnabus has put together a book where several different writers are describing their craft. In the second citation, editors Jones, Bailey, & Smith have put together a selection of writers all describing the importance of Andy Johnson on the writing world.

Barnabus, P. (Ed.). (1999).   *Writers and their craft.*   New York: McGoo-Hall

Laurel, P.T, & Bailey, B., (Eds.). (2003). *The impact of Andy Johnson on the writing of the 21th century.* New York: McGoo-Hall.

A Chapter in an Edited Book With One Editor

To cite the work of one author in a chapter in an edited book, the following information is listed in this order: (a) the author of the chapter, (b) the year published, (c) the title of the article, (d) the editor or editors (initials before the last name), (e) "Ed." in parentheses followed by a comma, (f) the book title which is italicized, (g) the page number or numbers in which the article is found in parentheses with a period at the end, and (h) the publishing information.

Curtain, J. (1999).   The importance of accurate citations. In. P. Barnabus (Ed.), *Writers and their craft* (pp 57-84). New York: McGoo-Hall.

A Chapter in an Edited Book With More Than One Editor

The only difference between this citation and the one above is that you would include *Eds.* instead of *Ed.*

McCormack, C. (2001). Using the objective stance in academic writing.

In. P. P. Keller, & K. Smith (Eds.), *Writing for success* (pp 102-149). New York: McGoo-Hall

Graduate Papers, ERIC, and Internet
Graduate Papers That Have Not Been Published
When citing a dissertation or a Masters thesis, the following information is listed in this order: (a) the author, (b) the year published, (c) the title which is italicized, (d) the status of publication, (e) the university, and (f) the location of the University.

Thoreson, E. (2000). *The affect of using direct instruction on the quality of writing in college freshmen.* Unpublished doctoral dissertation, Minnesota State University, Mankato Minnesota.
Lee, D.M. (1999). *Using whole language strategies in a freshman writing class.* Unpublished master's thesis, Minnesota State University, Mankato Minnesota.

ERIC
ERIC stands for Educational Resources Information Center. These documents are usually on microfilm, but hard copies are available also. Here, information is listed in the following order: (a) the author and year; (b) the title of the paper, italicized, capitalizing only the first letter of the first word; (c) the report number in parentheses [if any], (d) the city or state in which it was presented or published, (e) the conference or organization for which it was published, and (f) the document number.

Hanson, D.R. (1992). *Looking for intelligent life* (Report No. DSOS-A-282). Mankato, MN: Conference for Gifted Education and Talent Development. (Eric Document Reproduction Service No. ED 346 082)

Articles in an Internet-Only Journal
The purpose of the citation reference is to credit the author and to allow the reader to find that same document. To cite articles from an internet-only journal, the following information is listed in this order: (a) the name of author and the year, (b) the title of the article, (c) the title of the journal, italicized with the titled capitalized, (d) the place within the web site where it can be retrieved, (e) the date of retrieval, and (f) the web site.

Erickson, B. (2002). Meeting the literacy needs of gifted children. *Literacy for Exceptional Students, 2* Article 0003A. Retrieved April 12, 2002 from http://www.literacy.exception/jan/.html

Web Sites and Other Internet Documents

As stated previously, the quality of internet sources must always be questioned, as there is often not a review or jury process used in their selection.   However, sources put out by nationally recognized organizations such as the National Council for Social Studies (NCSS) or the US Department of Education might be considered. However, non periodical internet sources should be used with extreme caution. In these cases include (a) the name of the organization or web site, (b) the date of retrieval, and (c) the web site.

Literacy Lessons for an Inclusive Classroom. Retrieved January 12, 2002 from http://www.lessonplan.teachers.com

Citations in Action

The two imaginary articles below demonstrate how the authors use citations to build their cases. Even though both of them obviously have very strong opinions, they are able to state their ideas in a way that allows the reader to see the ideas and not the writer.

The Need for a Liberal Agenda
by Forrest Befree

Schools that have liberal, humanistic philosophies tend to foster better learning environments than those that are more conservative (Doo, 1969).   Fine (1994) found that humanistic schools created learning communities of high achievement, creativity, and nurturing. In a recent study it was found that those schools with a clearly defined liberal, humanistic philosophy had significantly higher college entrance rates than their conservative counterparts (Howard, 1992). It appears that this type of philosophical environment is needed in order to enhance learning and ensure a healthy society.

References

Fine, L.. (1994). Schools and achievement. *School Journal Quarterly,*
    52, 31-42.
Howard, M. (1992). Creating schools of higher achievement. *Journal of*
    Liberal Education, 78, 124-159.
Doo, S.D. (1969). Learning environments and student achievement.
    The Journal of Education, 46, 46-61.

The Need for a Conservative Agenda
by Malcom Wallace Applesbee Jr.

Schools that have a conservative Judeo-Christian philosophy tend to foster better learning environments than those that are more liberal (Welk,

1969). Duck (1994) found that conservative schools were more orderly, had low rates of vandalism, students were highly involved in community functions, and there were higher scores on achievement tests. In a recent study it was found that those schools with a clearly defined conservative philosophy scored significantly higher on college entrance examination than their liberal counterparts (Arbuckle, 1999). It appears that this type of philosophical environment is needed in order to enhance learning and ensure a healthy society.

References

Arbuckle, F. (1999). Keeping the status quo. *Convservative Quarterly, 49*, 157-178.

Duck, D.E. (1994). Creating an effective learning environment in our schools. *Journal of Liberty and American Education, 12*, 3-6.

Welk, L.T. (1969). *Ditto machines: The wave of the future*. Sheboygan, WI: Freedom Press.

Final Words on Citations

You will refer back to this page often. I would suggest you put a post-it note here. Also, you can get instant, on-line tips for writing, citing, and other aspects of academic writing at the following web site: http://owl.english.purdue.edu

Chapter 19

Quotations

Quotation Guidelines

Material quoted from another author's work must be reproduced exactly and cited within the text. You cannot copy phrases or sentences that somebody else has written and lead readers to think that they are yours. This is a form a plagiarism. A variety of quoting options are described and illustrated below.

Short Quotes Without Mentioning the Author

To state exactly what an author has written without mentioning that author's name within the sentence, enclose the author's words in quotation marks. This is followed by the author's last name, year, and page number all in parentheses. A period is placed at the end outside the parentheses.

"Fewer than 40 words, put the quote right in paragraph" (Author, year, p.123).

College campuses seem to be more tolerant of marijuana use. "Most college freshmen think that it should be legal to buy and use marijuana" (Johnson, 1995, p. 125).

College campuses are places where students are exposed to a variety of diverse viewpoints. "They are a melting pot of views and ideas, a great finger painting upon which ideas are pushed around, experimented with, and combined with unique effects" (Jones, 1993, p. 125).

Inserting Quoted Material into the Middle of a Sentence

To insert a quote in the middle of a sentence, list the author, year, and page number directly behind the quoted material. People usually do this if they want to use a snappy phrase that somebody else has written.

During the sixties, marijuana use among college students was "as common as backpacks and baseball caps are today" (Snidely, 1987, p. 45), and reflected the change in values and priorities occurring in society.

Short Quotes that Mention the Author

To state exactly what Zaar said and mention this name within the sentence:

Zaar (1995) stated that "most college freshmen think that it should be legal to buy and use marijuana" (p. 125).

Block Quotation

Block quotation is used if you have 40 or more words to quote. Here the quotation marks are omitted. Instead, you start a new line and indent the entire quotation five spaces. If you need to quote two or more paragraphs, new paragraphs are indented an additional five spaces. Block quotations are doubled spaced just like the rest of your paper.

> There is a wide diversity of opinion among college students on this issue. Most freshmen students think that marijuana should be legalized. In a recent survey 87.6% of these students stated that they believed people should be allowed to make their own choices; that marijuana is not any more or less dangerous than alcohol. If marijuana was legalized, it could be regulated and taxed.
>
> This position allows for more freedom and individual choice. It would also greatly increase tax revenues. The additional revenue generated from marijuana tax could be used to build new schools, hospitals, and transportation systems. Also, the legalization of marijuana would allow for regulation thus creating a safer product (Buchanan, 2001, p. 125).

Another Word of Warning

Just like citations, quotations should be used sparingly. You give away your authority if you allow your writing to become a series of *he-said-she-said*. Using citations is usually more effective than using quotes.

Writing That Lacks Authority: Jones (1998) believes that "choice is the American way" (p. 134). Smith (1981) said that "Freedom is the heart of our democracy" (p. 112). Frankel (1965) states,
> Freedom and choice are an integral part of what makes up our nation. We must believe in people's ability to make good choices. Without this belief, our government becomes a controlling parent figure. However, with freedom and choice comes responsibility. The question then becomes, How do we make sure that our students are able to make responsible choices? The answer is, by giving them instruction in and practice with making choices (p. 456).

Writing That Has More Authority: Choice is part of American culture (Jones, 1998), and an integral part of our democracy (Frankel, 1965; Smith, 1981). Providing instruction in choice making and allowing students opportunities to practice this skill will make them better able to make good choices in the future (Frankel, 1965).

The Reference Page

Just as with citations, the full reference citation for any quoted material must be listed in alphabetical order on the reference page. This allows the reader to identify your source.

Chapter 20

Quantifying Reality

When do you use numbers and when do you use words to express arithmetic concepts? The following information is taken from the Publication Manual of the American Psychological Association (2001). This is the manual that describes the style of writing used for writing in education, sociology, and psychology.

Using Numbers

Use numerals to express arithmetic concepts with the following:

1. Numbers 10 and Above -- The class generated 27 different ideas in the space of five minutes.

2. Dates -- This study took place on May 5, 1999.

3. Ages -- She is 7 years old.

4. Time -- The subjects reported to the laboratory at 1:00 P.M. They stayed there for 2 hours and 7 minutes.

5. People in a Study -- There were 15 students in this study: 8 males and 7 females.

6. Grade Level -- Most children begin grade 2 with a thorough knowledge of consonant sounds. (Note: It is grade 2 but *second grade*.)

7. Chapters -- Most would agree that Chapter 17 is the most fascinating chapter of the book.

8. Pages -- Page 1 of this text begins with a fascinating review of the writing process.

9. Scales or Rating Systems -- He scored a 7 on a 10-point scale.

10. *Money* -- The subjects in this study were paid $8 for participating.

11. *Numbers Grouped for Comparison with Other Numbers Ten and Above* -- The study showed that 9 out of 15 students were able to improve their grade averages significantly by learning how to read critically. Of the 15 students participating, 6 received A's, 5 received B's, and 4 received C's.

Using Words

Use words to express arithmetic concepts with the following:

1. Numbers Below Ten -- He sank three out of seven free throws.

2. Numbers that Begin a Title -- Mr. Higgins read the book, *Seven Silly Swans* to his second grade class.

3. Numbers that Begin a Sentence -- Fourteen children fell asleep during the story. (Try to avoid starting sentences with numbers.)

4. *Numbers Grouped for Comparison with Other Numbers Below Ten* -- In his reading class, seven out of the nine boys preferred action stories.

5. *Numbers in a Hyphenated Word* -- The Minnesota Vikings are four-time Super Bowl losers.

Reporting Numbers

There are four rules for reporting numbers:

1. Numbers are reported in descending order (from greatest to least).

Example: The mosaic contained 27 walruses, 14 elephants, 9 kangaroos, and 3 white-tailed deer.

In the example above, I begin using numbers instead of words (27 walruses), therefore, I had to remain consistent even though some numbers are below 10 (9 kangaroos and 3 white-tailed deer).

2. Tell what you are observing first.

Example: This study was designed to determine the types of movie genre that were popular among elementary students.

3. Report the total number before you report categories. Both the examples below are correct, however, the second one seems a little less repetitive.

Example: Out of 99 total responses, 47 preferred action movies, 31 preferred comedies, 14 preferred science fiction, and 7 preferred historical movies.

Another Example: Respondents in this study reported their favorite movie genre. Out of 99 total responses, the following preferences were noted: 47 action movies, 31 comedies, 14 science fiction, and 7 historical movies.

4. Stay consistent with the order of gender or other categories. Report numbers in descending order; however, when reporting gender or other categories, the order of the first example must remain consistent throughout.

Example: There were 28 students in the class: 14 males and 11 females. 9 males and 2 females were Caucasian, 3 males and 7 females were Black, and 2 males and 5 females were Asian.

Above, I started with the largest total category (Caucasian). The order here was 9 males and 2 females. In the following categories (Black and Asian), even thought the number of females was greater than the number of males, they were reported second so as to stay in a consistent order.

Tables

Tables are a quick, very visual way to organize and report information. They are especially useful if you have a great deal of numerical data to report and are meant to replace information written in the text. Thus, in the text, you might refer to the data or the conclusions, but do not duplicate table information in the text. For example, in a study looking at the leisure reading habits of high school students, I could put the following data in written form:

A study was conducted to determine the leisure reading preferences of high school students. Out of the 250 students surveyed, 140 were females and 110 males. The responses were as follows: action or adventure was preferred by 35% of the males and 5% of the females, mysteries were preferred by 10% of the males and 25% of the females, historical was preferred by 0% of the males and 35% of the females, biographies were preferred by 5% of the males and 25% of the females, fantasies were preferred by 20% of the males and 0% of the females, comedies were preferred by 15% of the males and 3% of the females, technical reading was preferred by 5% of the males and 10% of the females, and science fiction was preferred by 10% of the males and 2% of the females. Total responses were as follows: 40% preferred action or adventure, 35% preferred mysteries, 35% preferred historical, 30% preferred biography, 20% preferred fantasy, 18% preferred comedy, 15% preferred technical reading, and 12% preferred science fiction.

This is certainly correct, but it is not very easy to digest this amount of information. Below, a table is used to report the same information (see Table 20.1). For each gender, the preference is listed from greatest to least.

Table 20.1
Leisure Reading Preferences of High School Students

Males	Female
action/adventure - 35%	historical - 35%
fantasy - 20%	mystery - 25%
comedy - 15%	biography - 20%
science fiction - 10%	technical - 10%
mystery - 10%	action/adventure - 5%
biography - 5%	comedy - 3%
technical - 5%	science fiction - 2%
historical - 0%	fantasy - 0%

Use parentheses to refer to a table in the text (see Table 20.1). Since it is a title, Table is capitalized. The table number should be listed above the table, flush left. The title should be italicized and listed on the next line, also flush left, capitalizing the first letter of principle words. This lets the reader know quickly and easily exactly what is being read. If you are using chapters, break the table and figure numbers into chapters. Table 20.1 means Chapter 20, Table 1.

In Table 20.2 below, leisure reading preferences of high school students are again reported; however, the data here are grouped and listed in descending order according to the genre totals. (Note: Since I referred to Table 20.2 in the sentence, I did not have to put *"see Table 20.2"* in parentheses.)

Table 20.2
Leisure Reading Preferences of High school Students

Genre	Male	Female	Total
action or adventure	35%	5%	40%
mystery	10%	25%	35%
historical	0%	35%	35%
biography	5%	25%	30%
fantasy	20%	0%	20%
comedy	15%	3%	18%
technical	5%	10%	15%
science fiction	10%	2%	12%

Tables organize information and make it readily available to the reader.

Example: This study was conducted to see what kind of footwear middle school students wore. There were 117 middle school students observed for this study. The findings are shown in Table 20.3.

Table 20.3
Type of Footwear Worn by Middle School Students

Type of Shoe	Male	Female	Total
athletic or court shoes	25	20	45
hiking boots	20	21	41
sandals	10	20	30
dress shoes	5	6	11

Figures

Figures include lists, graphs, diagrams, or pictures. Figures are labeled differently than tables. The figure number is italicized, flush left, and followed by a period. The title of the figure follows and is not italicized. In the title, only the first letter is capitalized and the last word is followed by a period (see Figure 20.1). Figures are not the same as tables and should be labeled and counted differently. For example, I have used three tables thus far in this chapter, but this is the first figure so it is labeled, Figure 20.1.

Figure 20.1. Playground games.

```
1. Jump rope.
2. Soccer.
3. Playground equipment.
6. Football.
7. Chasing games.
8. Softball.
9. Other.
```

Graphs

Graphs are listed as figures. Bar graphs are used to show comparison. Most word processors have options that allow you to make high quality graphs quickly and easily (see Figure 20.2).

Figure 20.2. Bar graph.

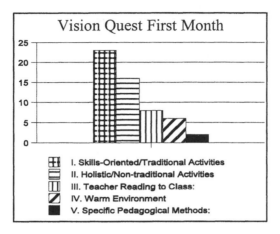

Line graphs are used to show change over time. Figure 20.3 shows how the types of responses changed over time.

Figure 20.3. Line graph.

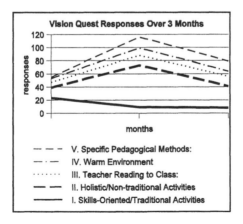

Other

Pictures, photographs, maps, illustrations, or sample products are all examples of figures and should be referred to in the same way as the figures described above. If you have an abundance of figures, they should be included in an appendix at the end of your report and simply referred to in the body of your text.

Reference

American Psychological Association (2001). *Publication manual of the American Psychological Association* (5th ed.). Washington, DC.

Chapter 21

The Literature Review

When reporting research or describing the application of a theory, you must first set the information in a theoretical context. This is done with a literature review, something that has been described in earlier chapters. A literature review simply reviews and synthesizes what the literature says about a topic, then reports it in an organized fashion. To do this you (a) gather sources, (b) read and take careful notes, (c) look for groups to emerge, (d) organize the data from your notes into sections, (e) create the first extremely rough draft, and (f) revise.

Sources

A literature review must be fairly extensive. Here the goal is to see what all the literature says about your topic and to become a knowledgeable expert. This expertise should be reflected in your writing. The number of sources used varies on the level and type of writing.

Sample of a Literature Review

Below is a sample of the first half of an article that was written to provide advice to choir directors for improving sight reading and music learning. Here, 12 sources are used to set this advice in a theoretical context.

Improving Sight Reading and Music Learning

There are many similarities between decoding alphabetic and musical text (Flemming, 1988; Johnson, 1995). Indeed, many literacy learning theories can be used to inform and enhance the practice of choir directors (Hodges, 1992). This article looks to put theory into practice, using theories found in literacy and learning to bring understanding to sight-reading and music learning.

Similarities Between Reading Words and Notes

Alphabetic and musical text both rely on a system where the reader must acquire a correspondence between a symbol and a sound with a left to right orientation (Adams, 1992; Hodges, 1992; MacKnight, 1975; O'Brubba, 1987). Both use symbols to describe thoughts or create ideas (Hodges, 1992; MacKnight, 1975). Music and literature both have technical aspects to master, but ultimately involve metaphors, feeling, rhythm, images, and structure (Gardner, 1985). Readers of both kinds of text need to master a basic set of rules (Flemming, 1988), however, these rules are best learned in the context of real reading and not as a set of isolated skills (Anderson, Hiebert, Scott, & Wilkinson, 1985; Beck & Juel, 1992; Boyle & Lucas, 1990; Goodman, 1986; Petzold, 1960). And finally, both music and literature involve passion, which can stir the soul as well as the mind (Flaming, 1988).

References

Adams, M.J. (1992). *Beginning to read: Thinking and learning about print*. Cambridge, MA: The MIT Press.

Anderson, R.C., Hiebert, E.F., Scott, J.A., & Wilkinson, I.A.G. (1985). *Becoming a nation of readers*. Washington, DC: National Institute of Education.

Beck, I.L., & Juel, C. (1992). The role of decoding in learning to read. In S. J. Samuels and A. E. Farstrup (Eds.) *What research has to say about reading instruction* (2nd ed.). Newark DE: International Reading Association.

Boyle, J.D. & Lucas, K.V. (1990). The effect of context on sight singing. *Council for Research in Music Education, 106,* 1-9.

Flemming, S. (1988). Beethoven, literacy, and me. *Language Arts, 65,* 661-668.

Gardner, H. (1985). *Frames of mind: The theory of multiple intelligences*. New York: Basic.

Goodman, K. (1986). *What's whole in whole language?* Portsmouth NH: Heineman Educational Books, Inc.

Hodges, D.A. (1992). The acquisition of music and reading skills. In R. Colwel (Ed.). *Handbook of research on music teaching and learning*, New York: Macmillian (pp 466-471).

Johnson, A. (1995). I was a less able reader: What concert choir taught me about reading instruction. *Reading Horizons, 35*, 430-441.

MacKnight, C.B. (1975). Music reading ability of beginning wind instrumentalists after melodic instruction. *Journal of Research in Music Education, 32*, 23-34.

O'Brubba, W. (1987). Reading through the creative arts. *Reading Horizons, 27,* 170-177.

Petzold, R.G. (1960). The perception of music symbols in music reading by normal children and by children gifted musically. *Journal of Experimental Education, 28*, 281-294.

Section Four
Science and Research

Chapter 22

Understanding Science and Research

As an academic writer, you will be using research to build and support your ideas. This chapter explores the nature of science and research.

Science is a Verb

One of the most basic human instincts is the drive to make sense of the world around us. This is the essence of science, the process of which has been going on in various forms long before there were words or written languages to record it. Science is not solely a body of knowledge or a particular content area, but a way of seeing, a process used to examine and organize our environment. Science, therefore, is a verb. To engage in the act of science is to look, ask questions, test questions, create order from chaos, find answers, and develop concepts.

Knowledge

While science is not a body of knowledge, it is highly dependent on having a well-organized knowledge base (Armbruster, 1993; Gallagher & Gallagher, 1994; Hodson, 1988; Johnson, 2000; Thelen, 1984). Knowledge helps scientists structure and assimilate new information. Science experiments are built upon accepted theories and previous research. New data make sense only when they are grounded in what is familiar. Thus, methods of science involve generating relations between the prior knowledge and new knowledge.

Science and Writing: A Harmonic Convergence

Both scientists and academic writers are involved in observing and making sense of the world around them. Gallagher and Gallagher (1994) list seven essential activities of a scientist. A scientist: (a) develops content expertise, (b) detects problems or asks questions, (c) observes, (d) organizes and classifies data, (e) measures, (f) hypothesizes, and (g) experiments.

Academic writers engaged in many of these same activities.

1. Academic writers develop content expertise. This is the information-gathering part of the writing process. Writers must have something to write about before they can write. This content area expertise is eventually displayed in the form of literature review.

2. Academic writers ask questions. Once writers have a topic, it should be put in the form of one or more questions. This helps to make information-gathering more efficient, as the writer is able to select only that information that pertains to the research question.

3. *Academic writers observe and classify data.* This is the stage directly after the note-taking. As described in previous chapters, once writers' notes are complete, they should observe, look for groups to emerge, and classify the data (the notes), by putting them into groups.

4. *Experiment.* Successful academic writers experiment by letting the data answer their questions. They also experiment with words, sounds, and phrases in order to determine the overall effect on the reader. This is part of the revising process.

The Nature of Research: Ways of Seeing

Research is a way of seeing. Research or re-search means to search again or to re-view things in a different way. The researcher is one who uses systematic observation as the lens through which to view a particular aspect of reality. However, research is one of many ways of seeing. Visual art, music, dance, drama, and poetry and creative writing are other ways of seeing which offer alternative ways of viewing reality.

Often people point to one study and say, *"Research says that . . ."* and then they insert whatever point they want to make. In this instance, they are attempting to construct reality using one research study. This is not quite correct. I sometimes hear others say, "Oh, you can manipulate research studies to make them say anything you want to." This also is not quite correct. The world is not black and white, neither is it a hodgepodge of colors thrown willy-nilly about. In this section I will attempt to explain the nature of research.

Like Sighting In a Deer Hunting Rifle

I am from northern Wisconsin where many people go deer hunting in the fall. Every year before the season, hunters sight in their deer hunting rifles to see if it is shooting accurately. If the scope has been bumped during the winter, the bullet will probably not go where the cross hairs indicate it should. One year as I was sighting in my rifle, it dawned on me that what I was doing perfectly illustrated the research process. My research questions were: Is my rifle shooting accurately? If not, what do I need to do to make it shoot accurately?

The next step was to collect data. I did this by setting up a paper plate at 100 yards, aiming for a dot in the center, and watching to see where the bullet hit. However, I could not rely on one shot to determine the accuracy of the gun. I may have wiggled or flinched when I shot. Thus, I took several shots until I noticed a pattern. There were holes in various places on the target, however, I began to see a cluster. This gave me a sense of where my gun was shooting. Each of the holes represented a bit of data. Had I taken only one or two shots, I could not be very confident of the accuracy of my rifle. This illustrates the importance of having an adequate sample size in any given study.

Each one of the holes appearing on the target as I shot was also like a research study (see Figure 22.1). While it may be possible to find research to support a variety of positions on any given question, one must look at the bulk of the research to begin to see the cluster. This is why it is important that a review of the literature be fairly extensive.

Figure 22.1. Research as target shooting.

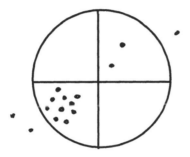

Experimental Research

Experimental research, sometimes called quantitative or empirical research, is where the researcher takes an active role in setting up an observation or experiment in order to isolate a variable. An independent variable is a factor that may or may not lead to a particular result, which is called the dependent variable (see Figure 22.2). This is the treatment or what you do to something or somebody. The goal of experimental research is to figure out what caused a particular effect or what the effect of a particular approach or treatment might be.

Figure 22.2. Terms for understanding quantitative research.

1. The *independent variable* is the treatment or factor that the researcher manipulates to determine a particular effect. It is what is done or not done to a group of people, animals, plants, or things.

2. The *dependent variable* is the particular result or the effect of the treatment. An easy way to remember the distinction between these two variables is to think of the dependent variable as depending on the treatment or independent variable.

3. The *treatment group* or experimental group is the group of subjects, participants, or objects that are exposed to the particular treatment.

4. The *control group* is a group as similar as possible in all characteristics to the treatment group, however, this group is not exposed to the particular treatment for the purposes of comparison.

5. The *research question* is that which the researcher seeks to find an answer for.

6. The *hypothesis* is a tentative statement that can be supported if the outcome of the experimentation is as expected. If there are a number of different tests which continue to support that hypothesis, it may be elevated to the status of theory.

7. A *theory* is an interrelated set of concepts that is used to explain a body of data. Most hypotheses never make it to the level of theory, as it takes a great deal of evidence to support it before it can be viewed as valid.

Isolating Variables: Causal or Coincidental?

There is a difference between things happening at the same time and one thing causing another. Coincidental variables (co-incidents) mean that two or more things occurred simultaneously. Causal variables mean that Condition A brought about Condition B. Beware of conclusions based on coincidental variables.

To illustrate a coinciding variable, when I was growing up the preachers on TV used to say that rock and roll music was the cause of moral decay and the increase in teen pregnancy. They noted that as rock and roll music became more prevalent in our society in the 60s and 70s, there was a rise in teen pregnancy. This was good sentiment but bad logic. These are coinciding variables. If one were to use this same logic, it could also be said that teen pregnancy caused rock and roll music to become more prevalent. Looking at all the variables operating in the 60s and 70s, it would be impossible to isolate rock and roll music as an independent variable for anything except maybe damaged ear drums.

An example of a causal variable would be cigarette smoking and lung cancer. Scientists have conducted controlled experiments and determined that cigarette smoking leads to increased rates of lung cancer. This was done by looking at thousands of laboratory rats in smoking and not smoking conditions. Also, thousands of smoking people were compared to thousands who did not smoke. (When using human subjects, a large sample size makes up for the lack of a controlled experimental environment.) The rates of cancer between these two groups were examined.

Shooting Baskets

Let me use another illustration to examine the process of experimental research. My friend Mary seemed to have a talent for making a basketball go through a hoop. I wanted to conduct some research to find out if she was a good shot. My research question was, "Is Mary good at shooting baskets?"

Mary always beats me whenever we play HORSE in the back yard, but this really does not tell me if she is a good shot or not. It could be that I am a very poor shot (which I am). Maybe she is able to make a lot of shots because the basket we use is very low. Maybe the rim is very wide. Maybe she is just extremely lucky. There are many variables here, thus, it is hard to determine with any degree of certainty if Mary is or is not a good shot. To do this, we went to a gym with a regulation backboard and hoop. She took a shot from the free throw line and the ball went in the hoop. However, at this point I still was not able to say that Mary was a good shot when compared to the normal population. This may have been a lucky basket.

Next, Mary took 19 more shots from the free throw line. She made 14 out of these 19 shots. Subjectively, I was impressed and thought this was very good, but my objective self said that the only thing I could state for certainty was that in this instance Mary was able to make the majority of her shots. She then took 30 more shots from the free throw line. In total, she made 30 out of 50 shots. I was able to conclude that the number of shots that went in the basket (30) was greater than those that did not (20). But could I now conclude that Mary is a good shot? Not according to my definition. I still do not know if this is better than the good. Maybe most people can shoot 30 out of 50 baskets.

The next step was to create a working definition of good. Here, good was defined as a basketball shooting score falling within the 85th percentile when compared to a normative population. Average was defined as a score within the 50th percentile, above average as a score within the 60th percentile, and excellent as a score within the 95th percentile when compared to a normal population.

To find these percentiles, I selected two thousand people at random from representative regions of the country and had them shoot 50 baskets from the free throw line. I counted the number of baskets that each made and created a standard. Mary's score was compared to the scores of this representative sample. It happened that she did indeed score better than 85 percent of those who took the shooting test. It was at that point that I was able to conclude that Mary's shooting performance was above average and thus, Mary is indeed a good shot.

But Wait ... Not so Fast ...

The shooting situation that Mary was in when she took the standardized shooting test was not a real situation. That is, we do not know if the results of this test transfer into an authentic basketball shooting situation. We might predict that Mary has a better chance of making a ball go through a hoop than someone scoring lower on the standardized shooting test, but in a basketball game there are many more variables such as reaction time, conditioning, opponents' ability, adrenalin, the defense, and your teammates.

If I really wanted to know about Mary as a basketball shooter, I would have to mix the quantitative data (scores from a standardized shooting test), along with a systematic observation of her in an authentic basketball shooting situation. This speaks to the fallacy of judging one's potential based on the standardized scores derived from academic achievement or ability tests. Those tests predict one's ability to do well in similar testing situations with similar test-taking kinds of problems, but the results do not necessarily transfer into real life problem-solving situations.

Qualitative Research

If I wanted to understand Mary as a basketball shooter, I would have to spend time observing her as she engaged in the act of playing basketball. This means going beyond numbers. In this instance, I would look at qualitative information or data that would describe the quality of that experience. Here researchers would not control or manipulate the environment, rather, they would observe the individual within the natural environment in a systematic fashion. The researcher here becomes the lens through which this bit of reality is filtered.

In Mary's situation, I would observe her on the basketball court during a game. To make this a systematic observation, I would decide which sorts of things to look for up front. In this case, I would create a chart to note the number of shots, the distance of each shot, and I would devise a way to record if it was an open shot or if there was an opponent with a hand in her face. I would also be able to observe and record the sorts of things Mary did to get open and the type of shots she made. All this data would help me understand Mary as a basketball shooter

Quantitative or Qualitative

Quantitative research uses numbers in order to know. Controlled environments are created in order isolate one particular aspect of reality. The questions are stated up front, and only the data that is related to the research questions are observed and recorded. A cause-and-effect paradigm is used to make sense of the world.

Qualitative research uses observations in order to understand. On a philosophical level, the qualitative researcher recognizes that one can never know completely. Here researchers take the world as they find it instead of trying to manipulate conditions in order to isolate variables. The questions are more open-ended and less defined with plenty of room to collect data through collateral observations

Is one research method "better" than the other? No. Both are to be used to answer different kinds of question.

References

Armbruster, B. (1993). Science and reading. *The Reading Teacher, 46,* 346-347.

Gallagher, J.J., & Gallagher, S.A. (1994). *Teaching the gifted child.* Needham Heights, MA: Allyn and Bacon.

Hodson, D. (1988). Toward a philosophically more valid science curriculum. *Science Education, 72,* 19-40.

Johnson, A. (2000). *Up and out: Using critical and creative thinking skills to enhance learning.* Needham Heights, MA: Allyn and Bacon.

Thelen, J.N. (1984). *Improving reading in science* (2nd ed.). Newark, Delaware: International Reading Association.

Chapter 23

Describing Empirical Research

When describing research studies, use one or two sentences to describe each of the following: (a) the question or purpose of the study, (b) the number and type of subjects, (c) the treatment or conditions involved, (d) the measure, and (e) the results and conclusions.

Vegetables
This section describes two studies related to vegetables.

Howard Study
Howard (1941) examined the effects of tomatoes on working memory. For this study, 40 subjects were chosen from a pool of 150 college students and randomly assigned to either a treatment or control group. The treatment group ate 3 tomatoes and the control group ate no tomatoes. Both groups took the Hawkins Memory Test as a post treatment measure. It was found that the experimental group scored significantly higher than the non-tomato control group in this measure. It may be inferred that tomatoes have some positive effect on memory.

Fine and Howard Study
Fine and Howard (1944) wanted to see if asparagus had any effect on reasoning ability. The subjects for this study were 168 adult selected from a shopping mall and randomly put into treatment and control groups. The Smith Reasoning Test was given as a pre-treatment measure and showed no statistically significant differences between the two groups. Over a six-month period, the treatment group was given 3.5 cups of raw asparagus to eat each day. The control group ate no asparagus during this time. Post-treatment measures showed no difference between the two groups.

Summary of Vegetable Studies
Here, the results of the studies reviewed are summarized.

1. Tomatoes have been shown to positively effect memory (Howard, 1941).

2. Asparagus has no significant effect on reasoning ability (Fine & Howard, 1944).

More complicated studies require greater depths of description, however, it is not always necessary to include every aspect of a study. For example, some studies may produce a variety of results, only one or two of which pertain to your particular writing topic. In these cases, report only the results that are of importance to your writing topic. And in your description, include only the information that is relevant to the results you are reporting.

Acquisition and Transfer of Thinking Skills Instruction
This section describes two studies which evaluate how thinking skills are acquired and transferred from one setting to another.
Robins and Mayer Study.
Robins and Mayer (1993) compared the effects of four instructional methods on students' ability to acquire and transfer analogical reasoning skills. Three identical experiments were conducted. The subjects were 93, 97, and 86 college students randomly assigned to one of four treatment methods.

A computer system was used to provide subjects with training on 20 practice analogies in one of four instructional methods: (a) schematic/high load, (b) schematic/low load, (c) non schematic/high load, and (d) non schematic/low load. The length and duration of each training program were not reported.

Schematic instruction consisted of practice problems grouped by type and accompanied by direct instruction which described the problem type. Non schematic instruction consisted of practice problems arranged in random order without a description of the problem type. High load instruction or problems that utilized a high cognitive load consisted of practice problems presented as exercises without examples of the correct solutions. Low load instruction or problems which utilized a low cognitive load consisted of worked-out examples which emphasized the formation of correct relational schemas.

After the training programs were completed, subjects were asked to solve new analogy problems of the same relational type (near or low-load transfer), solve new analogy problems of a new relational type (far or high load transfer), and take a recognition test of the terms from the previously presented analogies (recognition memory). Measures of students' error rates and response time were used to compare the effectiveness of each instructional method.

The results indicated that (a) schematic/low-load instruction was the best condition for learning problem solving initially, and for transferring this knowledge to similar or near-transfer problems; and (b) there was no significant difference in the types of instruction for problems considered far-transfer and for measures of memory recognition.

These results seem to suggest that thinking skills are best learned when the schema or problem type are identified and accompanied by direct instruction, the cognitive system is not overloaded, and there is an adequate amount of modeling and practice.
Schoenfeld Study.
Schoenfeld (1982) compared the effects of general problem solving

strategies or weak thinking skills to domain-specific strategies or strong thinking skills on the acquisition and transfer of problem-solving strategies. The subjects were college freshmen and sophomores enrolled in a mathematics problem solving course.

Control and treatment groups were used. Instruction for both groups was brief in duration but intense; students met for 18 consecutive weekdays for two and a half hours each day. Students' homework assignments for both groups averaged four to five hours daily.

The treatment group used class time to learn and practice general problem solving strategies in small groups, with an emphasis placed on the process of solving problems and selecting appropriate strategies. The control group used class time to learn and practice structured, orderly ways to approach problems. That is, they were taught domain-specific ways to solve problems without the emphasis on process and strategy selection.

Dependent variables consisted of analyses of fully solved problems, students' qualitative assessment of their problem solving, and measures of transfer.

In analyzing fully solved problems, researchers examined and compared students' ability to generate, select, and pursue plausible approaches to mathematical problem solving. The qualitative assessment consisted of a Likert-type rating scale where students reacted to their own problem solving performance and described their own problem solving processes. In assessing transfer, researchers used pre- and posttest measures to rate and record students' ability to transfer problem solving strategies to closely related problems, somewhat related problems, and unrelated problems.

Mean scores were compared without analyses of statistical significance. Pretest scores between the two groups were similar.

The posttest were as follows: (a) An analysis of fully-solved problems showed that out of 100 possible points, the posttest scores favored the experimental group with a mean score of 72.2 points, as compared to the control group's mean score of 24 points; (b) the qualitative assessment found students in the treatment group to be more organized in their approaches to problem solving, utilizing more deliberation and longer problem analysis and organization before attempting to solve problems; and (c) an analysis of transfer showed that out of 100 possible points, the posttest scores favored the experimental groups with a mean score of 86 points, compared to the control group's mean score of 13 points.

These results seem to suggest that general problem-solving strategies can be successfully used to acquire thinking strategies, and that these are more apt to be transferred to other situations when compared to domain-specific thinking skills instruction.

Chapter 24

Writing Using 3-D

As stated previously, writers must always assume the reader knows nothing. Therefore, when introducing a topic, concept, or skill which may be unfamiliar to the reader, use 3-D: Define, Describe, and Demonstrate. For example:

Define - Splandering is the practice of using power point presentations and behavior modification techniques to teach phonics skills to young children.

Describe - Here teachers identify a set of letter sounds and use power point to create visually attractive pictures to go along with these letter sounds. Behavior modification techniques are then integrated with the presentation in order to reinforce positive learning behaviors.

Demonstrate - During reading class children are asked to sit in chairs in an upright position with their feet planted on the floor. The lights are turned off and children are asked to focus on the screen in front of the room as the teacher begins the presentation. As the presentation begins, students are given sugar cubes every time they respond correctly to a power point prompt. If students give an incorrect response or if their attention drifts, they are given an electric shock.

Section Five
The Final Product

Chapter 25

Theses and Dissertations

This chapter describes the parts of a Masters level thesis and a doctoral level dissertation. Colleges and universities all have varying requirements for these. Make sure you know the specific guidelines for your institution before beginning.

Some Survival Tips

The survival tips presented here will help facilitate the process of writing a thesis or dissertation. Some of these are a review of things covered in earlier chapters.

1. See your advisor before beginning your graduate paper.

2. Give yourself plenty of time to complete your project. Graduate papers take a great deal of thinking time and revising.

3. The goal is to create a professional paper that contributes to the field.

4. Your advising professor will provide feedback and some editorial comments, but an advisor is much different from an editor. The onus is ultimately on you to write in a logical, coherent, objective style.

5. First identify a problem or decide on a topic for research, then put the problem or topic in the form of a question or questions.

6. Create a preliminary outline for your topic or question using an inverted triangle which goes from most general to most specific.

7. Plan on revising each chapter a minimum of four times.

8. Assume the reader knows nothing.

9. Stay objective.

Secondary Research

Secondary research uses data gleaned by others in the form of journal articles and other academic sources to answer a research question. These projects have four chapters.

CHAPTER I
INTRODUCTION

Keep this chapter as short as possible (three to eight pages in length). Start with the introduction to the topic (no heading for this section). Identify the problem, provide background information, and connect to the larger world.

Problem Statement

Use a centered heading. State the problem and the purpose of the paper.

Example: The purpose of this paper is to review current literature related to writing workshop and to describe effective implementation practices.

Then, put the purpose in the form of one or more questions.

Example: The specific research questions are:
1. Is writing workshop effective in developing students' writing skills?
2. If so, how should writing workshop be implemented in a middle school setting?

Importance of the Study

Use a centered heading. Tell why the project is important and to whom.

Example: The information here will be of value to . . . It will also provide elementary teachers with a plan to . . .

Methodology

Use a centered heading. Tell how the data were selected. What were the criteria?

Example: Data were collected using nationally recognized, academic journals. Each journal was peer-reviewed and printed no earlier than 1996. Texts written by recognized experts in the field were also used.

Limitations of the Study

Use a centered heading. Describe the limitations or applicability of the results. Can it be applied only to a certain segment of the population? Were you able to look at all facets of the problem?

Definition of Terms

Use a centered heading. Briefly define the important terms the reader will encounter in the review of the literature.

Headings. Use third level headings for each term (Italicized, indented five spaces, a capital letter on the first letter of the first word, a period at the end, and begin the description on the same line).

Description length. Descriptions are in glossary form and are one or two sentences in length. Complete sentences should be used here.

CHAPTER II
REVIEW OF THE LITERATURE

This chapter contains a review of the literature related to your topic as described in this book. This is the heart of the secondary research project. Include only information that is necessary to answer your research question. Create structure using headings and subheadings. Include empirical research in order to support a particular application. This chapter ends with a brief summary of the major points covered. This summary can be in list form or described in one to three paragraphs.

CHAPTER III
APPLICATION

Select and synthesize relevant information from Chapter II to create an application. Your application should answer some or all of the following questions: What are your recommendations? How should this knowledge be used? What is your plan? What should it look like? How should it work? How might others use it? Do not include new information here, rather, use only ideas that are based on information presented in Chapter II. Assume the role of the expert. Use headings and subheadings to create structure. Cite when necessary.

CHAPTER IV
SUMMARY AND CONCLUSIONS

Keep this chapter short (three to eight pages in length). Start with a short review of the purpose of the paper and restate the research question or questions. No heading is used for this first section.

Summary

Use a centered heading. Summarize the important points from Chapters II and III. The presentation of ideas here should be in the same order as they appear in Chapters II and III. These may be in list form or described in one or two short paragraphs.

Conclusions

Use a centered heading. Describe the specific ideas or conclusions you have as a result of the information found in Chapters II and III. Explain the implications of the findings to other situations, populations, and education settings.

Recommendations

Use a centered heading. Describe your recommendations or how the information should be used. This should be a brief restatement or overview of your application from Chapter III. Note that Conclusions and Recommendations sometimes merge into one section.

REFERENCES

Reference citations are listed in alphabetical order by authors' last names. Do not include extra spaces between citations.

APPENDICES

Appendices are not required. However, they may be used to provide the reader with more detailed information that would be distracting to read in the main body of the article. No commercial material may be included here.

Original Research

Original research uses an experiment or some form of systematic observation to create and collect data. This data is then used to answer specific research questions. These projects have five chapters.

CHAPTER I
INTRODUCTION

Start with the introduction to the topic (no heading for this section). Identify the problem and state any general questions related to the area of inquiry. Also, provide a sense of why this inquiry is important.

Background Information

Use a centered heading. The title of this heading should be related to the background information you are providing. Although you may have as many as three sections here, it is important to keep this chapter as short as possible. Provide only enough information to help the reader understand the problem or question and put the purpose of your study in a meaningful context.

Purpose of the Study

Use a centered heading. In one sentence, describe the purpose of the study. Then describe the subjects or participants, treatment or conditions.

An example for a quantitative study: The purpose of this study is to investigate the effects of thinking skills instruction on students' writing. The sample consisted of 167 elementary students assigned to one of two groups: an experimental group in which classroom teaching implemented thinking skills lessons and a comparison group that received no treatment. This study explores whether thinking skills instruction improved students' ability to generate and organize their ideas for writing.

An example for a qualitative study: The purpose of this study is to investigate middle school students' use of humor. The researcher spent six months in a suburban middle school near Minneapolis that had 356 students in grades six through eight. Data were collected using field notes, student interviews and surveys, and teacher interviews. The researcher wanted to explore students' use of humor in negotiating their social, emotional, and academic worlds.

CHAPTER II
REVIEW OF THE LITERATURE

This review of the literature begins the same as secondary research. Use academic books and journal articles to build theoretical context and describe research studies that can support or inform your question, hypothesis, or problem statement. It ends with the research questions.

Statement of Specific Research Questions

Use a centered heading. This section states your research questions and, for quantitative studies, describes the measures used to answer them. These are at the heart of the study as everything that follows is designed to answer these questions. Be concise yet specific here.

An example for a quantitative study: This study will seek to answers four questions:

1. Will thinking skills instruction demonstrate a significant effect on students' ability to generate ideas for writing? This will be measured by comparing scores and change scores on students' prewriting samples.

2. Will thinking skills instruction demonstrate a significant effect on students' ability to organize their ideas for writing? This will be measured by comparing scores and change scores on the Jones Holistic Writing Assessment (Jones Assessment Company, 2002). Student and teacher surveys and interviews will also be used here.

3. Do students perceive thinking skills instruction to be useful? This will be measured using a Likert-type rating scale to assess students' attitudes and perceptions. Student and teacher surveys and interviews will also be used here.

4. Do teachers perceive thinking skills instruction to be effective? This will be measured using a Likert-type rating scale to assess students' attitudes and perceptions. Student and teacher surveys and interviews will also be used here.

An example for a qualitative study: This qualitative research will seek to investigate three areas:

1. What kind of humor do students use? What are the humor related topics? Who are the subjects of the humor?

2. In what situations do students use humor? How do the delivery and content of humor change from varying situations?

3. What are the social, emotional, and academic contexts of humor? Is there an aggressive element in humor? Are there varying purposes for the use of humor?

CHAPTER III
METHODOLOGY

This chapter describes the subjects, materials, procedures, and the design and analyses used in your study. Past tense is used to describe all aspects of methodology.

Subjects, Sources, or Participants

Use a centered heading. The title of this varies according to the type of study. Quantitative and qualitative studies are described differently. For more information related to the nature of qualitative research, read *A Short Guide to Action Research* (Johnson, 2002). Describe the humans or materials. If humans are used, the reader should know the age, where they came from, how they were chosen, number, and gender breakdown. If humans are not used, describe what is being examined. Also included here is a description of the setting, conditions, or environment in which the study takes place.

Materials

Use a centered heading. Describe any materials used in the study. This may include materials used in the treatment as well as any measuring or data collection devices such as rating scales, rubrics, field notes, or survey instruments.

Procedures

Use a centered heading. Describe how the study was organized and conducted and how data were collected. This should be a recipe for your study written in such a way that another person could read and replicate it. Describe the treatment (for quantitative studies), and how you went about collecting data.

Design and Analysis

Use a centered heading. For quantitative studies, identify the independent variables and the dependent variables. For qualitative studies, describe the conditions. For both, describe the experimental design and tell how the data were analyzed.

CHAPTER IV
RESULTS

This chapter presents the results of the study. Since research happens in a specific instant in time, use past tense to describe all results. Listed here are just the data or facts. Conclusions or inferences related to these are usually saved for the last chapter. Use tables and figures as necessary. Create a centered heading for each question and describe the results below.

An example for a quantitative study: Will students receiving thinking skills instruction demonstrate a significant change in their ability to generate ideas? This was measured by comparing scores and change scores on students' prewriting samples. The data were analyzed using a 2 x 2 analysis of variance with the variables being the two treatment groups. The analysis of variance for the writing scores is shown in Table IV.1.

An example for a qualitative study: What kind of humor do students use and what are the topics and subjects of this humor? The type of humor most often used by these middle school students was the sexual reference and word play. Table IV.1 shows the types of humor and the frequency of their use. Table IV.1 also shows the difference in gender with males using more sexual humor while females used more personal attack humor . . .

CHAPTER V
DISCUSSION
This chapter contains an overview of the study, a summary of results, conclusions, limitations of the study, and recommendations or practical implications.
Overview of the Study
Use a centered heading. Restate the purpose of the study and briefly describe how the results were obtained.
Summary of Results
Use a centered heading. Provide a brief summary of the results. Present these results in the same order as they appeared in Chapter IV.
Conclusions
Use a centered heading. Move beyond the data to tell what the results mean and describe possible implications. Using subheadings, organize the conclusions around each research question.
Limitations of the Study
Use a centered heading. Describe the research goal and any limitations of the study. That is, what data might have been missed by the design? Based on this, describe limitations for the application of the results.
Recommendations
Use a centered heading. Describe how the results might be used or applied and provide ideas for future research.

REFERENCES AND APPENDICES

References and appendices for original research are presented in the same way as with secondary research.

References

Johnson, A. (2002). *A short guide to action research.* Boston, MA: Allyn and Bacon.

Chapter 26

Journal Articles

This last chapter provides some tips related to writing for publication, specifically, journal articles, however, the information here can be used also by those wanting to publish other types of expository, philosophical, or how-to articles in journals or magazines.

1. Make sure you have something to say. It is very easy to spot an article that seems to be written simply to be published. The best articles are those where the writer truly has a significant idea, a point of view, or some research to share with others.

2. Short articles are more likely to be published than long articles. There is limited space in most publications. Also, shorter articles will generally get more careful attention from editors and reviewers. For most academic journals, aim for 8 to 15 double-spaced pages plus references.

3. Choose the right journal or publication. Spend time initially previewing a variety of publications to see if your article is a good fit. Many journals describe the mission statement or general philosophy inside the front cover. It is futile to submit an article to a journal that has a mission statement that does not support your topic or point of view.

4. Read the submission requirements carefully. Journals usually ask for three to five copies to be sent. Sometimes return envelopes or postage is also required. Make sure your article aligns with the required format. The most common formats are APA, MLA, or Chicago Style.

5. Spend a great deal of time writing, revising, and getting feedback before submitting. Articles that are rushed contain many organizational, grammatical, and other types of errors. This demonstrates academic sloth and makes it less likely that your article will be considered favorably by the reviewers. Also, find a valued colleague to review your article and provide honest feedback. This will enhance the likelihood of acceptance.

6. Use reviewer feedback to grow. Sometimes it hurts to read reviewer feedback, however, this is the best way to grow as a writer. Do not take it personally. While you do not have to agree with all the feedback, realize that the editors and reviewers are the gatekeepers who decide whether your article gets published.

7. Revise and resubmit. Getting rejected is all a part of the game. The best writers get rejected. There are many academic journals and other types of publications. Continue to revise and submit, and your article will eventually get published.

Index